LAUGH

& Get RICH

How to Profit From Humor In *any* Business

LAUGH & Get RICH

How to Profit From Humor In any Business

Rick Segel & Darren LaCroix

Specific House

Laugh & Get Rich

How to Profit From Humor In Any Business

published by:

Specific House Publishing
One Wheatland Street
Burlington, MA 01803

Copyright © 2000, 2001 Rick Segel & Darren LaCroix
First printing 2000
Second printing 2001, revised
Third printing 2002
Fourth printing 2004

Requests for permission should be sent to:

Specific House Publishing
One Wheatland St.
Burlington, MA 01803
781-272-9995
781-272-9996 (fax)

Printed in the United States of America

ISBN: 0-9674586-0-9

Table of Contents

About the Authors

Rick Segel, Certified Speaking Professional (CSP), a seasoned retailer of 25 years, is an internationally awarded speaker, trainer, and consultant. He has delivered over 1200 presentations and has challenged and delighted audiences in many different industries—from baking to banking, retail to manufacturing, and the corporate world to government. He is the author of *Retail Business Kit for Dummies*, *How to Drive Traffic to Your Business*, and has authored two retail training videos. Rick is also the on-line marketing expert for Staples.com.

For more info about Rick see www.RickSegel.com

Darren LaCroix is a corporate comedian and a nationally known keynote speaker. He is the founder of The Humor Institute and teaches speakers, trainers, and sales people *how to be funnier!* His client list includes IBM, Fidelity Investments, Sheraton, and numerous national associations. Darren is featured in films, commercials, and training videos for companies such as Konica, Dunkin' Donuts, and EMC² Corporation.

For more info about Darren see www.DarrenLaCroix.com

Preface

Laugh & Get Rich

How to Profit From Humor in Any Business

This collection of tools will serve as your blueprint for business success while you enjoy the process. Humor makes "cents." We are living in a user-friendly, instant-gratification, entertain-me-now society that is willing to part with its hard-earned money—if the process is made entertaining.

Quality, service, and selection no longer differentiate a business. If you don't have those things you're not even in business any more. The question is, how do we differentiate ourselves so that our businesses can become memorable and a top-of-the-mind resource? The use of humor in business is powerful because it not only attracts new business and keeps existing customers or clients, it also makes the process enjoyable for our employees.

Good, hard-working, dedicated employees have become an endangered species. Is the *Laugh & Get Rich* philosophy the wonder drug for business today? YES! This book shows you how to make this way of thinking part of your corporate culture.

Acknowledgments

I, Rick Segel, would like to dedicate this book to three special people

First, to my brother-in-law Lenny Liss. Lenny is a Traffic Engineer who openly admits to being boring and nerdy and is proud of it. Ask him how business is and he replies, "There is always traffic." Those are the same words he has been using for the last 30 years. I have never gotten Lenny to laugh. I think he does, I just don't know when.

Yes, Lenny, this book is for you. When you read this, use your old slide rule as a bookmark.

Second, to my wife Margie, my life partner in everything I do. She is my friend, confidante, soul mate, girlfriend, lover, and most trusted advisor. We met when we were both 15 and we got married at 21. We have three of the greatest kids in the whole world, all of whom are married, and we feel as if our life is just beginning. Without Margie's love and support, this book would never have been written.

The last person I want to dedicate this book to is my mother, Sara "Ruth" Segel. She was the true inspiration for this book. The reason is simple—she lived the *Laugh & Get Rich* philosophy. She was brought up as poor as poor can be. She left home at 15 to find fame and fortune, only to have her father die tragically in an automobile accident, and she became responsible for raising her four younger brothers and sisters. She went on to own one of Greater Boston's most successful woman's specialty shops. When she died, she was a success, both financially and personally, with a smile on her face, loads of laughter, and two or three great stories or jokes at the ready for the appropriate moment. She didn't just do business, she had FUN. She was way ahead of her time. She never knew that what she did was right, but right it was. Mom, thanks for being the role model to follow and an inspiration to so many.

This book is especially for all the humor-deprived, analytical types who are reading this and saying, "You mean that if I use this humor tool I will make more money? How many laughs will it take and what is the formula?" And of course they want to know, "Where is the proof? Where is the documentation? Where is the instruction manual?"

Darren LaCroix would like to thank

Rick, for asking me and believing in me enough to help him with this fascinating project. We had too much fun during our writing sessions.

All of the executives who allowed us to interview them to give this philosophy credibility and a reality check.

Rosalie & Roger LaCroix, my mom and dad, whose love and support allowed me to pursue my dreams of comedy, speaking, acting, and now writing.

Brian Tracy, CPAE, whose words of wisdom, "What would you dare to dream if you knew you couldn't fail?" changed the course of my life.

Jane Conway who stood by me when everyone else thought I was foolish.

Rosemary Verri, the funniest woman I know, and the person who introduced me to professional speaking.

Izzy Gesell, who was a huge support in my earliest days as a speaker and helped me through the tough times.

Dave Swartz, a colleague who badgered me (at my request) almost every day because he wanted to read this book before he passed from this life.

To friends who came around, and people who told me I couldn't do it (sometimes you have to have the carrot and the stick).

To Dave Fitzgerald, Alan Weiss, Ph.D., Marie Weiss, Stanley Ralph Ross, Greg Godek, John Docimo, Glenn DiTommaso, Jon Yates, Tanya Field, Katie Grady, Jon Sneider, Renee Kaspar, and Rita Schiano.

To managers who helped me to pursue my dreams, and stay employed—Cindy, Ed, Al, Robin, and Bruce.

Thank you to God and St. Jude—miracles do happen.

The book is now in print!!!

Rick and Darren would like to jointly thank

Our editor, Chris Roerden, who was quick, precise, and made us look good. We also cannot forget Jim Weems and his crew at Ad Graphics for their tireless efforts. You were a true pleasure to work with.

To those we have overlooked, we'll get you next time around!

"Humor is one of the most under-utilized tools
in business today. It unlocks the riches for those
who seek to tap its power."
– Darren & Rick

Introduction

Why a book about laughing and making money? No, our goal is not to turn you into professional comedians. Instead, we are going to train you in the under-utilized tool of humor—humor, which can add profits to your bottom line by doing two of the most basic things in any business: increasing sales and reducing costs.

We all run out to buy products we see advertised on TV. Why? Because those ads make us want those products. How do companies do that? The companies make us laugh, they make us remember, and they make us feel as if they and their products are part of our lives.

Why us, Rick and Darren, as authors? You've heard of Shock Jocks? We won't go that far, but we won't give in to political correctness, either. Our purpose is to change the way you think about humor as a tool for bottom-line business results.

Rick Segel has been a retailer, retail consultant, and speaker for over 30 years. He has learned to appreciate the power of humor and how it can make the cash register ring. Rick has shared his rather offbeat philosophies with more than 1,000 audiences throughout North America.

Darren is a professional comedian and corporate keynote speaker. He also works with companies to bring humor to their corporate training videos. Darren, along with Rick, spent four years interviewing corporate executives and business owners who use humor as part of their business strategy.

Who is this book for? Which department of a company is the most important (besides yours)? Without sales there is no production, but without advertising there might not be sales. Without shipping there is no distribution, without research and development you are selling old stuff. Without accounting there are no invoices or receivables, but without credit there isn't any money coming in…and on and on. The overall success of any company is dependent on every department, even if you are in business for yourself. Each part of a company is equally important, which means that humor is needed in every department, though perhaps in different ways.

Humor is the great social lubricant that helps us function more effectively, the same way grease and oil help to lubricate the inside of a car to make it run smoother and work more efficiently. For some of you, this book will be an oil change with a good additive. Others out there are like tin men, dying for even a drop of oil to get them on their Yellow Brick Road. Without the oil of humor you might get left behind!

By the time you finish this book you will know how to humorize your own business without having to spend millions on the project. (That is, unless you want to, in which case, you may call us any time. We will not sell out for money, but you could rent us. If we make this complicated enough you might just call us in to humorize your business. So as you read this book, please don't take any notes or write anything down that could help you. We don't want you to be too smart. Do you know what consultants are charging nowadays? We could be rich.)

Back to our topic at hand—the purpose of this book. We want to help you harness the power of humor and increase your competitive advantage in this highly competitive marketplace. If a stuffed rabbit can help sell millions of batteries, think what a humorous attitude can do to increase your influence with your customers and employees? To this end we explore the ways humor affects the way we do business and the way we buy as consumers.

This book is set up in a format to let you see the different tools you can use, the ways others have used them, and the insights from others who have already improved their businesses using humor. Some of our examples have even used humor as the foundation for building their businesses. This book is designed to generate ideas in your head on how to improve your bottom line with the power of humor, not to spoon-feed the ideas to you. Of course, some of our examples may not relate directly to your business. These examples were chosen because they actually happened to us. Look for the universal principles within the stories, and you can make the lessons your own.

So—we are off to see the Wizard of Business, the Grand Pooh-Bah of Humor, on our Yellow Brick Road that is full of danger from those witches of the west who only laugh sinisterly and say, "You can't laugh at work, my pretty! Stop laughing and fooling around and get to work!" We believe the real work occurs when you are fooling around and laughing toward a goal. This is how to achieve your goals and enjoy the process. (If you are enjoying the process, aren't you more likely to reach any goal?)

We are going to teach, educate, and basically have a good time while sharing our somewhat off-centered way of looking at the world of business: the fun way. In the words of the great humor guru Joel Goodman, "(Fun) is where the bottom line meets the laugh line."

Laugh with us while we explore the philosophy of the power of capitalistic humor. We are here to talk about making money with the awesome power of humor and laughter. We are talking about the tool of humor, the tool that makes life worth living, work more fun, and money fly into your business. Humor has the power to turn red ink into black.

As the Great Hong Ling Soo once said, "An enjoyable journey of a thousand miles begins with one laugh." (You can catch Hong Ling at some of the comedy clubs near Peking.) Let's begin our journey to prove that fun is not the opposite of work, but that fun and work go hand in hand. Get your bucket full of laughter and let's melt the witch!

PART I

WHY HUMOR?
...THE BENEFITS

CHAPTER 1

What Were You Thinking?

Why did you pick up this book?

---

*"It's the humor influencers in life
that make us buy!"*

– Rick Segel

There are thousands of book titles out there. Why did you pick this one? What thoughts went through your mind? Perhaps you thought this one could be interesting? Maybe you believed this is a book you'd actually finish. Could be you have some experience with how humor works and want more. Did this book simply look like a fun thing to read? Or—are you just a money hungry capitalist and proud of it? (We are!)

Think about how the title of this book made an impact on you. How do you think you and your marketing goals make an impact on your potential customers? Think how those goals would be affected by the use of humor or even a hint of humor. You don't have to hit your clients over the head, just make 'em laugh or smile. Even half-smiles work for those hard-core, laugh-deprived individuals. There, we just succeeded in teaching you the first lesson of humor. It affects you and the way you spend your money. Humor and fun SELL.

This first lesson is worth the price of the book if it gets you to start looking at the rest of your buying decisions and start analyzing how the use of humor and fun affect the way you spend your money. When we started to analyze how we spent our money, a large percentage of those decisions were influenced by humor. From choosing the battery in our flashlights to having lunch at Wendy's, we made decisions influenced by humor. Start tracking your own "humor influencers." We think you'll find humor influences you the same way the lights of Las Vegas affect the mood of gamblers—by enticing them and grabbing their attention. Is that the message humor gives you?

This first lesson was the expensive one. It represents the entire cost of the book. The rest of the lessons are free! Doesn't that make you feel better? The rest of the book is simply our added-value gift, free for reading the first chapter. Enjoy! If you would like to send us something for our generosity, we love cannolis!

RECAP: (This is where you participate, take notes, and increase your learning.)

- What were your thoughts when you first saw the title of this book?

- What goes through your customer's or employee's mind when fun is involved?

- How can humor and fun help to sell your products?

- What are your humor influencers—the things that make you buy?

Ideas for your business: (This is where you participate and increase your sales.) It's your book; you can write in it if you want to.

CHAPTER 2

The Humor Benefit Program

100% coverage with extended care

"Life does not cease to be funny when people die any more than it ceases to be serious when people laugh."

– George Bernard Shaw

What are the benefits of humor? Why should we all strive to add humor? How many benefits are there? We have grouped the benefits into 10 categories, and when you finish this chapter it will be obvious that you should be using humor whenever possible, and then some. Let's get started with the number one reason (according to our research and the experience of everyone).

Humor Benefit 1: Listening!

People are more likely to listen to your words if they are entertaining and informative. How many times have you heard the statement, "You're not listening"? Why does this happen? Two reasons. First, the listener is preoccupied with his or her own concerns. When Rick's wife asks him a question about taking out the trash, letting out the dog, or any other humdrum activity, Rick tends to tune her out, especially if he is listening to the scores from last night's games on TV. Rick's wife is fighting for his attention against a force more powerful than the message she is offering.

The second reason people aren't listening is simple: the message being delivered is boring. It puts people to sleep. Not only is the message boring, but also the delivery is so mundane that no one wants to listen. A common pet peeve among humorists is the hiring party that is "too serious a company" to hire a humorist.

Humor allows a message to be delivered in a more palatable manner. Most people eat cereal, but how many would eat it without the sugar and sugar substitutes put in and on each bite? Not many, especially kids. And what are adults if not just older kids? As you will read in "The Poppins Principle," it's the spoonful of sugar that makes the message go down. That chapter is about the importance of humor in training, but the same rules apply here. What you say must be said in an interesting manner to first get an audience's attention and then to get them to listen to what you are communicating.

Are there other ways of making what you communicate interesting? Sure, but humor is the simplest, the cheapest, the most under-utilized-in-business, the most universal, and the most common denominator to masses of people. Ever watch a mime perform to an audience made up of different cultures? Everybody laughs and enjoys. When you see other people laugh, you start to laugh. It's contagious.

Benefit 2: May I have YOUR ATTENTION PLEASE?

Humor gets your attention so you can listen. Getting an audience's attention really comes before listening, but it doesn't have the long-range power that listening has.

Here's what happened to Rick recently. He had a speaking experience in which everyone expected to leave the function at 2 P.M. However, the meeting planner did not introduce Rick until

1:56 P.M. Rick was supposed to do a 30-minute spiel, but because of the time, his speech was cut down to 10 minutes. The audience was already hostile because instead of being able to network and share stories with each other during lunch they had been bombarded with winning raffle announcements (complete with the emcee's repeatedly saying, "Could everyone please be quiet").

By the time Rick hit the stage, they'd had it! When the meeting planner began to deliver Rick's standard introduction, Rick stormed the stage and interrupted his own introduction. This was different. It was out of the ordinary. Speakers normally wait to be properly introduced, then start. But the last thing this audience needed was protocol.

In order to get an audience to laugh, you have to first get their attention. The key was to use the element of surprise and speak in the mindset of the audience. Rick's quick evaluation of the audience's mood and capturing of their attention by acting in an unexpected manner (but one appropriate to the situation) put the audience in a listening mood and set them up for his message.

That is what we want you to do. Put your listener into a listening mood. It works in the same way that a talk radio station requires fewer advertising spots than a music station. When you listen to talk radio you have your listening skills tuned in that much finer. You don't tune into talk radio for background ambience. Some think the ratio between talk radio's effectiveness and ad spots required is a minimum of 2 to 1, but many music stations believe that 3 to 1 is even better.

The point is, if your mind is elsewhere it takes much more effort to capture your attention. Why waste time? Keep your audience alert with different and interesting attention-grabbing techniques, and the use of humor is the best. It keeps listeners in the listening mode. That's why many music stations break in with yelling, screaming, or even the occasional dig or jab. It's all just to get the audience's ears back into the listening mode.

Here's a quick review. Humor gets attention and has your audience listening. We use the term "audience" because of Billy.

Shakespeare, that is. He taught us that all the world's a stage. Therefore, every person you wish to communicate with is your audience. Whether you are a speaker, a manager, or a company CEO, you have to communicate your message in order to accomplish your goals. That includes every medium of communication: telephone, fax, e-mail, regular mail, meetings, and conversations on the golf course. You are performing to your audience, and that requires you to use the skills you have learned so far. First, getting people's attention through humor, and second, using that humor to keep them listening.

Benefit 3: Do you remember when we___?

We can all fill in that blank. "Do you remember when we stayed up all night for client XYZ and got so slap happy?" "Do you remember the time the boss started the meeting about new requisition procedures with her slip showing and she was trying to be so serious?"

We remember things in conjunction with other associations. If you take any of the popular memory training classes, that is the technique they are teaching. Associate the things you want to remember with other things that you already remember. One example uses your living room furniture placement, left-to-right, to remember the points of a speech. If your sofa were the first object on the left, you would associate the first thing you had to remember with the sofa. If your speech discussed dairy farm cows and your first point was cow health, you might picture a cow lying on the sofa, the remote control in one hoof and a can of soda in the other. If your next living room object is the door to the kitchen and your next point is the effect of a cow's health on meat production, you might next picture the steaks in your freezer. And so on.

In some classes they call these things memory pegs while others refer to them as NLP (Neurolinguistic Programming). Whatever you call them, it's all about remembering things by association. Humor is the most natural and powerful way of creating associations for increased memory. Any memory course will teach you that the more outrageous the association, the longer the retention. Every humorist learns that if you want to make a point, wrap it in a story. People will think about the story and remember the point you are trying to make.

Aesop was really big at that. He had a fable for everything, and look how long his stuff has been remembered! Imagine growing up with Aesop as your father. "Dad, I don't care what the moral is, can I have the keys to the car or not?" Sure, you cynics are saying, "Aesop's stuff wasn't all funny." You're right, but can you imagine if it was? He would be even more famous than he already is. His listening potential would far out-rank Disney's.

We are using old Aesop to add a little humor to this chapter and to help you remember. We are trying to create a memory association with the use of humor.

What do we talk about at work? Someone is always talking about some funny commercial on TV that made them laugh. They never talk about the boring or dramatic commercials. "Still going." That tag line is quoted by more people every day because everyone has seen it and REMEMBERS it. Think about it—we are quoting someone else's sales promotion!

What about the Maytag Man? To drive home a point about dependability and quality, Maytag shows us a repairperson sitting around all day doing nothing! We are a country going through a period of downsizing and elimination of corporate waste and they pay a guy who does NOTHING. We think it's funny and we get the message. Think of the poor guy who had to come up with a funny commercial about washing machines. We bet he wasn't laughing when he walked out of the meeting with that assignment! But he succeeded and everyone remembers the Maytag brand. Name any other company delivering as effective a message as Maytag and most likely they are using humor.

We will be exploring the use of humor in advertising in later chapters, but if you want to have someone remember what you are saying, give them a humor anchor to hold on to. Humorous stories cement the retention value.

Benefit 4: The social lubricant

Friction causes pain, so add a lubricant. What do we mean? Humor is the new common denominator in business. It is the social lubricant that separates the polished businessperson from the rest of the pack. It is the oil that helps an engine run smoothly; it helps that polished businessperson make you feel comfortable. It makes awkward situations bearable. It establishes the parameters to social behavior, with the possibility of true bonding if humor icons match. For example, while probing, you discover a common favorite comedian in Robin Williams. That common interest is a good basis for a relationship to begin.

Tell a funny story. Ask an audience who their favorite comedian is. What was the last comedy they saw? Forget about talking about the weather: talk about comedy or humor. Find out what makes your audience laugh. That is the secret key to finding out what makes them tick. How do you find out? Ask them. People love to talk about what makes them laugh and they do it with a smile. How many times would you have given anything to get someone to smile? Do they like clowns? Do they like slapstick? Are they into political humor? Do they like blue humor? (Blue humor is very risky, and cries lawsuit, but in certain groups it can create a strong bond.)

You can tell a lot about a person by what they laugh at. An unforced laugh is truth to the soul. Why are we wasting time trying to find out if it's going to rain tomorrow or guessing what the temperature is going to be? Think *humor!* Think small talk. *Think humor!* Think networking.*Think humor!* Think bonding. *Think humor!* When you think your boss is a jerk. *Think humor!* When you don't know what to say. *Think humor!* When you are depressed. *Think humor!* When employee morale is down. *Think humor!* When you think miracle drug. *Think humor!* When you first meet. *Think humor!* When you think humor, *THINK DOING MORE BUSINESS!*

We could go on and on, but we have to go the bathroom now. (Not really, we were just trying to be funny.) See, you don't have to be uproariously funny to utilize a form of humor. Johnny Carson made a fortune telling lousy jokes. He always had great savvy for the joke. He is the greatest "goalie of comedy."

To the new executive who is reading this book, lighten up! Being serious is a typical rookie mistake that separates the seasoned pro from the "wannabe." Remember, it is the humor of the situation that makes all the parts work well together. The piston and the cylinder are both made of steel, but without that oil, both parts don't work well together. There is just too much friction. Don't let your cylinders get scored. Let humor remove that friction to make your organization run smoothly.

Always have a cute story in your back pocket ready to use. Not offensive, just something that is timely and appropriate for different occasions. Maybe something about your child or a pet. Have something that can help create a friendly atmosphere in which to do business. Your ice-breaking line should always be light and funny; it will help to unwrap the layers of nervousness and hostility. You want to change the business environment to upbeat and fun. Fun sells. We will repeat that line 1,000 times throughout this book. It relieves the pressure from difficult situations and people.

Which brings us to the next benefit: stress reduction through humor. However, if you start off with humor as the social lubricant instead of with a serious demeanor, the need for stress reduction is itself reduced.

Benefit 5: Tension relief & stress reduction

How do you spell relief? H–U–M–O–R. This is based on the Minnifield Principle of Humor, which states that you cannot be stressed or angry when you are laughing. The simple test developed by Dr. Minnifield is to hold on to the side of your chair or grasp something as tightly as possible. Then, at the moment of maximum stress and tension, try to laugh. When you laugh, all the tension leaves your body. Stress and laughter are two emotions that simply cannot occur in the human body at the same time.

At the beginning of his speaking career, Darren presented his Humor Workshop at a conference in Boston. When he arrived at the hotel he turned his car over to the valet and struggled up the stairs with his visual aids. (Presenting brings with it an anxiety all its own.) Darren was planning to show 200 nurse practitioners how to add humor to their presentations. He had hired a videographer to capture the magic moments on the platform, but the man was nowhere to be seen. With only 10 minutes to go before the program was set to begin, Darren discovered that his notes were missing. They were in the car, so Darren proceeded to retrieve them. When he got to the valet he learned that he had to be escorted to his car. Ready to go once again, Darren discovered he'd also left his audio music tape, his big opening, in the car. He rushed back to the valet and asked to be taken to his car, again. After the tape was retrieved, the valet noticed the tension on Darren's face and said in a thick Asian-American accent, "Next time you come, we park your car closer?"

Darren broke down laughing. All of his tension was immediately gone! Which makes it much easier to present humor. Did the valet have to say anything? No. Did what the valet say make a difference? Yes. Did Darren give him a big tip? Of course not! It was the beginning of his career and he couldn't afford it (though he did greatly appreciate it). It changed Darren's mood and made his presentation more effective than it would have been without that tension breaker. He cannot begin to tell you the night-and-day difference those simple words made in his career.

It doesn't take much to be effective with humor. All it takes is that one timely piece that can turn a situation from doom and gloom to outrageous laughter. Can this be helpful in business? Yes! Especially when someone makes a mistake. It's the great cover-up that doesn't slide the mistake under the carpet, but brings it forth and laughs about it at the time it happens.

The humor formula by Steve Allen is "Tragedy + Time = Comedy." Sometimes you can move up the time sequence to receive a small amount of humor relief. Just like the valet did in Darren's situation.

Rick tells a story on the platform about a woman who came into his clothing store to buy a dress for her daughter's wedding. It was expensive, if you consider $500.00 to be expensive for a dress. The woman insisted that her daughter's hem be sewn by hand, with no stitches showing. This is an old-fashioned way of doing a hem, very time-consuming and obviously very costly. When the woman came into the store to pick up the dress, she was mortified to see a machine stitch on the dress, every stitch showing. This woman and her daughter went ballistic. She called Rick every name she could think of and wanted to know how stupid the people were that worked in the store.

This was not the time for any type of humor. Rick gave the customer three choices. First, the store could refund all her money right then and there. Second, they could order a brand new dress and redo all the alterations. Or, third, the woman and her daughter could have a seat and wait for the dressmaker to redo the hem. If, after the dressmaker redid the dress, the woman was not satisfied, she could still choose the first or second option. The woman agreed to option three but was still very unhappy. She took a seat near the dressing room with her daughter, and you could see the steam still coming from her ears.

After about five minutes, two young women came into the store. Suddenly one of them began to have a grand mal seizure right in front of the dressing room area. Rick ran to the dressing room to check out the situation and observed that the person having the seizure was starting to rip off her clothes. This was a time for professional help, so Rick ran to the phone to call for medical assistance. When he passed by the woman waiting for her dress to be re-done he said, as he kept walking, "I don't know what the trouble with her is. We didn't shorten her dress."

After the ambulance left and the woman's dress was finished to her satisfaction, she said to Rick, "Was I really that bad?" Innocently Rick answered, "Yes," and then proceeded to remove the tension from his reply by adding, "I deserved it." It was that well-placed line that became the tension-reliever, just as the valet's line did for Darren.

Humor has power. It's natural and cheap. It builds professional relationships. Rick works on thinking funny during difficult times just to change his mood and point of view.

Benefit 6: Bonding—Getting close for comfort and profit

Ever crack a tooth? Immediately you lose the piece of tooth. Then you go to the dentist with this chipped tooth right in the front of your mouth and the dentists says she can fix it. What does she do? She bonds it with some foreign substance, dentist glue or whatever they use, and *voilà!* Your tooth has been bonded. What does this have to do with humor? Nothing, but it's late in the day and Rick went off on a tangent when he read the word "bonding." He figured you would expect a very pungent tie-in. Oh well, here it comes. Brace yourself!

Any business is only as good as its parts. If a company has a strong sales force but poor manufacturing, the best customer service policies will work only so long. A company without R&D is doomed (Rick and Darren?...no Research and Development), and eventually it will get caught by the competition and be left by the wayside. Businesses today understand the team concept. Everywhere you go, there is always some company using the expression TEAM _____ (insert any company name here). Everyone from Xerox to Hertz to Dollar Tree Stores to Bose® is using teams, and people must bond to create that proper team chemistry.

What's the natural bonding substance? You guessed it: humor. It brings people together. When was the last time you shared a good side-hurting, makes-you-cry belly-laugh with someone? It's as good as sex. Well, maybe as good. A special feeling occurs between two people who share laughter. That is why sometimes when you watch a stand-up comedian on TV and the people in the audience are laughing uncontrollably and you think, "Ehh?" It's because the members of the audience have bonded with the comedian and bonded with one another as well.

If everyone around you is laughing, you are more likely to laugh. At home, if there isn't anyone laughing with you, the comic is only so-so. When cable became prevalent and stand-up comedy was on every channel, it meant the end of the '80s stand-up comedy boon. People thought watching it was the same as being there. It is not. Put eight people in the room and now there is an audience that will bond while they laugh together.

Our friend and past president of the New England Speaker's Association, Valla Dana Fotiades, intentionally sets up her seating arrangement in a horseshoe shape. She does this because the audience members are able to make eye contact and see the reactions of others in the group. This causes them to bond. When two people share the same emotional reaction, it brings those two people closer. Humor is the second best form of bringing people together. The first is tragedy. But there is already enough of that in your organization and community, so why not try humor?

As we said earlier, humor is the great social lubricant to get things running smoothly, and it is also the great social super-glue that creates powerful bonds that can last a lifetime. The best part about this entire philosophy is that it is done softly, silently, and invisibly. It is one of those rare elements of chemistry that has no properties of its own, but aids in the performance of other elements of life and business—bonding people together and spreading without a conductor.

Benefit 7: Escapism

What we're talking about is better than drugs, is habit-forming, and practically free. "Hi, my name is Darren, and I'm a Humor-o-holic!" Audience responds, "Hi Darren."

Humor can be a positive addiction. It has the same effects that many of the best-selling drugs have, but it's a positive addiction. It makes us forget the frustrations of our daily lives. It's the mini-vacation, the break in the humdrum routine of the day. It's the 4:45 P.M. feeling when you look at your watch and say, "Where did the day go? It wasn't like being at work, it was just fun."

Rick recently picked up an Ambassador Christmas card that read, "Merry Christmas...working with you is such fun...[open the card]...I sometimes forget that I'm in Hell."

The mind can really focus on only one thought at a time, and if we fill our mind with fun and humor, it makes us feel good even if we are surrounded by negative influences. How many times have you heard someone say, "I love working with Jane—she is so much fun to be with!" That person generally takes the focus away from the problem at hand to a productive but party-like atmosphere.

Why do we go to a movie? Why do we go to a show? Why do we tell jokes? Why do we listen to jokes? Why do we pay so much for entertainment? Why do lottery tickets sell so well? Who makes more money: Barney or schoolteachers? If you're not sure about this one, they aren't merchandising dolls of any teachers I know of. We listen on the evening news every night about murders, violence, and even layoffs and downsizing. These days we live in a society that's saying, "Stop the world I want to get off"— but we can't. Even vacations aren't guaranteed to be any less stressful than the work environment we've just left.

Humor provides us with a complete distraction from the humdrum and can make the humdrum worth living. Look at some of the best situation comedies on TV. Sitcoms are about everyday life; they simply look at that life from a different point of view. From *The Honeymooners* to *All in the Family* to *Married with Children* to *Seinfeld*. These are all merely slice-of-life situations that make people think about their own situation's being not as bad as they might have thought. This is escapism at its best.

Why does a coach take a player out of a game? To rest and get rejuvenated. The coach knows that with some rest the player can go back into the game refreshed. Humor is like a Gatorade for the game of business. It refreshes the worker so he or she can be more productive. It even beats a coffee break because you can still work while humor is taking place (and there is no chance of spilling it on your keyboard.)

In the words of Sherwin Greenblatt, CEO and president of the Bose® Corporation, a leading innovator of sound reproduction technology, "There is no reason why you can't relax, laugh, and do the things that one considers play while you are working. I think that's the healthiest and best mixture. We certainly have enough stress that we can use some fun and play." So the next time the troops are low, tired, or sluggish give 'em a fix. Let them get high on humor!

Benefit 8: Be user-friendly

What's more friendly than humor? Ten years ago we didn't even know what the term user-friendly meant. It was new to our vocabulary—one of those new high-tech terms. Now, everyone uses it. It has become a standard phrase for the computer software industry. Up to that time we thought all computer nerds were speaking a foreign language. Then came the Apple Macintosh, and everything changed as the emphasis shifted to making technology easy to use and understand. By making technology easy to use, understand, and less intimidating, the computer and other technology industries realized they could attract more of a cross-section of the world. The dream of a computer in nearly every house is becoming a reality. Icons started to be fun, and directions were written in a playful manner. Manuals even included asides to the users to let them know the company understood how they were feeling.

In 1995 the great Microsoft introduced Windows '95. Other than the wonderful new things it could do, it was introduced to make an IBM or a compatible PC user-friendly. Microsoft wanted to make this boring piece of equipment warm and fuzzy.

That's what humor does to the workplace—it can make it a warm and fuzzy environment. Let's face it, company loyalty is not what it used to be. "Downsizing" is the new hip expression for getting rid of employees. If a company doesn't downsize, Wall Street thinks the company is not keeping up with the times. Humor has the capability to revitalize employee loyalty to the company or to the job.

If you wake up in the morning and look forward to going to work because it is going to be an enjoyable experience, chances are you'll perform better and not call in sick. You might hate the company and your boss, too, but if the environment is upbeat and playful, you overlook those obstacles and work hard without even realizing you are.

One of the best examples we could give you is our experience of being actors in improvisational, interactive wedding shows. The owner of the company is okay with only limited loyalty to the cast because he believes there are hundreds of people who would love to be part of the cast. He is right about that. So every actor is always on his or her best behavior when the owner is around. We all know we are only a mood change away from getting replaced. However, doing the show is so much fun and the other members of the cast are so much fun to work with that we tend to overlook the things that might ordinarily upset us. The show itself is very user-friendly to the actors performing it and to the audience receiving or buying the performance. It always reverts right back to the cus-tomer—they have the ability to read us like a book. If we are down, they know it. No one wants to do business with unhappy people. This is just good sound business.

Make your work environment user-friendly. It works well internally and externally. Putting a smile on an employee's face will get transferred to your customers, and that makes for more business. That's what this is all about—making the register ring. So even if you hate your employees, make your company user-friendly, down to the computer screensavers you use. When workers walk by a computer screen showing Opus or any of the other creative characters, it puts a smile on their faces and gives your company that user-friendly feeling.

Benefit 9: Acceptance

Hey, the new guy is okay. The easiest way for a new employee to fit into a company is to share the company humor. Acceptance skyrockets when fellow employees feel that a new person is part of the team. The easiest way to become part of the team is to share laughter. There's that bonding feeling again, but this time the purpose is to have the new person feel comfortable and welcomed.

We have all experienced employees who do all the right things but are never accepted because they don't share in the office humor. People believe that the new person is stuck up or conceited, or that the new person sees him or herself as better than the rest of the department. This does not help the team concept.

It works the same way when a new supervisor or manager is brought into the company. Everyone is on pins and needles until they meet the new boss. If the new supervisor uses humor or shows signs of a sense of humor, the supervisor can almost gain instant acceptance with a quick retort, quip, a funny memo pad, or any other form of humor.

Darren landed a speech for American Express Financial Advisors from a woman who kept his "humorous" fax pad from a speech two years earlier! We do not say this because his ego needs feeding; we say it because it works. His first speech was good. The woman loved the fax pads, too. Without both, Darren would not have addressed the financial advisors.

Your employees do not have to like you to get the job done—just respect you. We think it is that much better if they *like* and respect you. It makes a huge difference.

Humor is merely a shortcut to gaining acceptance from our employees, co-workers, superiors, and even people we carpool with. It's the icebreaker whose time has come to be recognized as a powerful tool in the business world. Why aren't business colleges teaching courses about humor and its value as a tool to productivity? (We are working on changing this, by the way.) Humor is a part of human nature that should be a part of everyone's arsenal of weapons in waging the business wars.

Benefit 10: Brainstorming

Anyone out there have a good idea? It has been our experience as professional speakers and seminar leaders that when you ask an audience to split up into groups to solve a problem, giving them the wildest and craziest instructions sparks the most creative answers. The groups start with their minds going off on crazy tangents and that somehow triggers more creativity than if you just tell them to solve the problem. However, if you tell them only to solve the problem but within the group is the class clown, that group comes up with better ideas than a group that does not use humor in its creative thinking process.

The class clown rarely comes up with the winning idea but usually stretches the boundaries of the group, expanding the group's paradigms. The whole idea of brainstorming is to get the creative juices flowing to come up with an innovative solution. There are many books and workshops on the brainstorming process, but we are concentrating on humor power. Dr. Roger Andersen, president of Adirondack Community College, shows a 10-minute video of the comedian Carrot Top, an extremely creative prop comedian, before his groups begin. What a powerful and enjoyable idea. It works!

The point is, when you get people to think funny, you are getting them to *think*, and how many times do we say to our employees, "Just think!" Again, humor serves as that social lubricant to get people into a thinking mode.

The other week Rick had an interesting thing happen that demonstrates this point. Rick is responsible for finding space to house New England Speaker's Association (NESA) meetings. He has had problems finding space that is both convenient and reasonably priced. He was speaking to a fellow NESA member about this problem and joked, "I guess we will just have to buy a building and rent out the space when we don't use it." The other person, also a humorist, replied with a little bit of disgust and indignation, "Was that supposed to be funny?" Rick replied, "Lighten up! I'm only trying to brainstorm. My best ideas come from the absurd."

Then it hit him—why not contact all the companies in the area that might have meeting space to rent out on a Saturday? Same idea, just reversed to NESA's being the renter instead of the owner. NESA did not buy a building. However, the thought did open an interesting avenue that would never have been explored were it not for Rick's absurd comment. What was discovered is that many of the buildings for sale are also places that can be rented. Usually, the more outrageous an idea, the better the practical solution will be that comes out of it. So the next time you need to brainstorm, call the class clown. It works.

RECAP (make notes — it's your book)

- Benefit 1 Listening!
- Benefit 2 May I have YOUR ATTENTION PLEASE?
- Benefit 3 Do you remember when we___?
- Benefit 4 The social lubricant
- Benefit 5 Tension relief & stress reduction
- Benefit 6 Bonding—Getting close for comfort and profit
- Benefit 7 Escapism
- Benefit 8 Be user-friendly
- Benefit 9 Acceptance
- Benefit 10 Brainstorming

Ideas this gives you for your business:

_____

_____

_____

_____

_____

_____

_____

CHAPTER 3

Accepting on Behalf of Productivity... It's Humor

Gaining acceptance starts at the top

"Accepting a new concept is the toughest part of change."

– Rick Segel, 1955

Where does it all begin? For humor to become a part of a company's business philosophy it starts with the acceptance of humor by the company's upper management. Do they buy into the concept that humor works? Do they understand that the company can be more profitable with the use of humor? Many companies let you joke or play but believe that business must be serious.

Recently, Rick had the opportunity to interview with a major consulting firm in Boston. It wanted to hire a humorist to train its people in upbeat, positive networking, using the power of humor as effectively as possible.

The company knew that with the right types of tasteful humor this would work well. However, the concept of using humor was so foreign to its corporate culture that the firm elected to hire someone who was content-driven, not at all a humorist. Too bad. The people with whom Rick interviewed were not upper management. They were well-paid, middle-management types with a good idea but ultimately afraid that such a risk might cost them their jobs. Rick sensed this in the middle of the interview process (selfishly, because no humorist/trainers want to be where they are not welcome). So he stopped selling himself and made a referral in the middle of his presentation. Because of the company's conservative nature, that other person eventually got the job.

Here is the irony of the whole situation. This is a firm that does controlled growth consulting. In other words, before companies think about growing, they call this firm, whose staff of Harvard eggheads tells you how to grow. Sadly, this company is missing the boat on one of the most powerful tools any company has: its own natural humor.

This firm's attitude toward humor is simple: there is no room for frivolity in business. To think that they are management consultants on growth! The person who interviewed Rick said, "The people here are wound too tight." Rick's automatic response was, "If humor adds to productivity, then why, as management consultants, would you not want to use or at least explore the power it possesses?" The interviewer answered with a look that said, "I believe it, but if I were to sell that idea, I would be laughing all the way to the unemployment line."

Darren and Rick would officially like to thank people like that. They are the individuals who will be left on the stoop when the revolution begins. If it weren't for people like them, there wouldn't be a need for us, the Heroes of Humor! Lighten up! Get a life! Chill out! Watch your register ring. To all our friends at that Boston consulting firm whose names we carefully excluded, remember this: a person who does all the right things with a sense of humor will out-produce the person who does all the right things without a sense of humor.

Innovation is using a foreign concept and making it mainstream. For every major idea that was ever proposed, someone said, "It can't be done." All of them: the TV, the microwave, the computer, and the glow-in-the-dark chair. You've never heard of the Glow in the Dark Chair Company? That's because they listened to the people who said it wouldn't work.

Many people agree that humor works in business, but they are still afraid to use it. It's not that foreign an idea. It is similar to the zipper, which took 40 years to gain acceptance after its invention. The zipper had the same problems as humor—no one took it seriously, and the mainstream was afraid to use it. Humor has to be controlled and used effectively, and its limits must be understood.

It all starts with your attitude toward embracing the humor concept, allowing humor in the work environment knowing it must be controlled and focused toward growth (just like atomic power must be controlled and focused). Be prepared to allow mistakes to occur. In any new concept they will happen, but keep your eyes on the big picture.

Here is the bottom line. All of this can be filtered down to one simple concept: "laugh and ____." (Insert any word here. May we suggest learn). Accepting this concept is more than just lip service. You must believe that humor has its place in business and that it results in sales and profitability.

RECAP:

- Be willing to accept the idea that humor works to aid in productivity.

- Acceptance is the horse not the cart....

- There are plenty of companies that refuse to buy into this concept, but you no longer have to be one of them.

- Be willing to accept mistakes in humor as in any new concept.

- Humor must be controlled like the ATOM.

- Remember the Glow in the Dark Chair Company, because no one else does.

Ideas this gives you for your business:

CHAPTER 4

The Humor is Coming, The Humor is Coming

Jump on or get run over!

"The most effective learning is accomplished during periods of fun and enjoyment."

– Ralph Smedley,
founder of Toastmasters International

L ast week, Darren and Rick spoke to The Association of Accounting Professors. This group was wild! Watching grass grow was probably more exciting. Our message to them was simple: add humor to the classroom and your students will pay more attention, remember more, and have more fun.

We spoke about using humor in the classroom, and all the professors agreed that it is definitely the thing to do. We even showed them the brochure from The Accounting Game, a company that uses the concept of accelerated learning to take dull and boring topics and add high doses of play and fun, making the learning more palatable. To attend The Accounting Game is also much more expensive per hour than to attend college, but it promises two things. First, it promises an understanding in one day that's equivalent to a six-week bookkeeping class. Second, it promises to be a fun place where the learning is entertaining.

The sad part about our experience was that most of the accounting professors practically pooh-poohed The Accounting Game concept as trivial and childish. Why? Is it that most preferred the tried and true and were too conservative to experiment? Shame on them.

Standard accounting textbooks compound the professors' conflict between agreeing with us (that humor in the classroom is good) and their dismissal of The Accounting Game theories. There is only one word to describe these books: boring! They are not user-friendly—as if the people who wrote them said, "I had to learn it this way and so do you!" Wake up guys and smell the coffee. It is not a sin to have fun while learning.

If the goal is the transfer of knowledge from one person to another, then as many techniques as possible should be used. Some people are auditory learners, some are visual learners, and many are kinesthetic. Some love to learn with story, others just want the facts. But whatever way people like to learn, most love to be entertained while learning. It works better for all concerned. If teachers had figured this out a long time ago, maybe society would be paying them at the same scale as entertainers.

We love the similarities between teaching and the Revolutionary War strategies. The British wore red coats and had to be organized, orderly, and proper because "that was the way it was done." They knew about guerrilla tactics but chose not to use them, because the civilized military just didn't do that. They did the right thing, which in retrospect was the wrong thing. Isn't that what these accounting professors are doing? They are doing the wrong thing, all the while thinking it's right because it's tradition. It is time to start breaking traditions and focus on the goal: transferring knowledge. This is a war of the mind, and all is fair in love and war. Let the games begin.

RECAP:

- The more entertainment, the higher the levels of learning.
- Traditions fall hard.
- Concentrate on the goal, not the way it's always been done.
- Any subject can be made fun, even accounting.

Ideas this gives you for your business:

_____

_____

_____

_____

_____

_____

_____

_____

_____

_____

_____

_____

CHAPTER 5

Boring Just Doesn't Sell

Is your business boring? It doesn't have to be

"A jest often decides matters of importance more effectively and happily than seriousness."

– Horace

In a recent issue of *Home Office Computing*, Charles Koshell IV is quoted as saying, "Sometimes we get accused of trying to entertain people into buying. But nobody can be bored into buying anything."

Mr. Koshell is the executive VP of Cliff Freeman & Partners, the advertising agency that created "Where's the beef?" for Wendy's and "Pizza! Pizza!" for Little Caesars. These ads grab our attention, and in this world of thousands of images that bombard us on a daily basis, any tool that can grab one's attention (even for a split second) is a worthwhile tool. Getting a potential customer's attention is 90 percent of the battle.

How does humor in advertising help sales? Humans associate laughing with being among people they know and like. We get a comfortable feeling about a product because our subconscious can't differentiate between laughter when we are being sold and laughter with our closest friends.

Our brain processes only the laughter; the purpose of the laughter comes much later in the thought process. Humor researcher Izzy Gesell is currently testing this concept. He has tested people's "humor response level" trying to find out why people laugh. The reasons for what makes different people laugh are as diverse as our tastes in food. What Gesell is discovering is that the mind does not differentiate between the origins of laughter. In non-technical terms, a laugh is a laugh. It is the same with natural or synthetic motor oil. Your car engine doesn't know one from another. Both make the car run. Your mind doesn't know a commercially induced laugh from a natural occurring laugh. The benefits of laughter remain the same, and your body and mind like it a lot.

What we realize is that if you associate your product or service with laughter or fun, you create a lasting laughter association with your product. The warm fuzzy feelings and properties of the laugh become intertwined with the image of your product. Humor becomes the celebrity endorsement, with the celebrity being laughter. Just as Charles Koshell IV associated Wendy's and Little Caesars with fun in their ad campaigns, you can do this with your company or product by simply associating it with humor.

This point is becoming more and more important in our complex world because personalities are becoming market niches. The way a company acts, who they do business with, the causes they support, even the fonts of their advertisements and the tone of their copy writing creates a base of customers or followers—or pushes potential customers away. Competition is so keen that slight differences affect the marketplace. Who would have thought just a few years ago that the concept of cause-marketing would spawn companies the size of The Body Works, Ryka, or mutual funds that are groups of environmentally concerned companies. The way a company acts is now a determining factor in whether or not to do business with them. That is why humor in advertising and positioning is becoming so powerful. But the company must also back up that created image with the same positive feelings throughout the company.

Adopting a fun advertising slogan is just the beginning. It must be reinforced with fun and humorous techniques on the front lines to be true to your advertising. Why give a mixed message? Don't you just love going to see your friendly banker? The problem is that they usually aren't very friendly face to face, so the term "friendly banker" has almost become an oxymoron. The key to reaching greatness is consistency throughout an entire organization. Savvy consumers quickly discover when a company's humorous outside is just a front for a boring inside.

Ask yourself the Number 1 question in everything you do: "How can we humorize this step or process?" Not all ideas will work and not all steps will be easy. Some will take time to humorize. But just by asking the question you will become a hero within your organization because your employees will believe you care. And with humor, you really will!

RECAP:

- Boring doesn't attract.
- The origins of laughter can't be differentiated.
- A company's attitude creates a personality that attracts customers.
- Consistency in humorizing adds the difference.
- Get the celebrity endorsement of laughter for your product or service.
- Laughing on the outside but crying on the inside is quickly discovered by savvy consumers.

Ideas this gives you for your business:

CHAPTER 6

The Clown Concept

It ain't all about red noses and big feet

"Everyone tries to be different in the same way."

– Rick Segel

How do you feel when you see a fully made-up clown? We're not talking the class clown or the company clown. We're talking a white-grease-paint, turned-up mouth, red-nose, big-feet, polka-dotted and oversized-pants, silly-hat, white-gloves, horn-blowing, wig-wearing type of clown. Do you feel HAPPY? Does a smile come on your face when you picture this clown? You bet it does. Why? Why does someone acting like a silly fool make us happy? Why does it make us feel good? Why does our attitude change? Is it a sense of freedom that the clown is acting the way we would love to act, but we are afraid of how others would judge us? Or does it bring us back to our childhood and all the fun things we used to do before we were told not to do them?

Do you get the same feeling when you go to work every day? If you are working for the right company you probably do. But for

35

the thousands of others who still work for the unenlightened companies, you can only dream.

The clown makes us laugh and makes us feel happy. Why? Who cares why! It works—don't fight it. Do you know the principles of aeronautics? No. Do you fly in airplanes anyway? YES. We are not here to research why a clown makes us laugh. Just accept it and let it work for you.

So what's with the clown? How do you use the Clown Principle and how does your company profit from it? Do you think Ronald McDonald was a bad idea? Sure he appeals to kids, because kids love to laugh. But so do adults. Having an image associated with laughter and love is never a bad idea. Even if you are a bank or a securities firm. We would rather do business with a company that has the ability to laugh at itself rather than with an organization that frowns at the idea of humor in business or doesn't laugh at all. I want to do business with people who are real.

Even when McDonald's started building homes for parents of kids who are hospitalized, they stayed with a consistent theme by calling the homes Ronald McDonald Houses. The sound of the name is less threatening just because of the association with a clown. Do you think the original idea was a fun concept or a brilliant marketing plan? We believe it was both.

Recently, Rick was at a humor conference in upstate New York and noticed a chunky little clown there. Most of the attendees at the humor conference wore casual clothing, and only 10 or 12 wore clown costumes. This little clown stayed in her clown costume the entire weekend. Any time you passed by her you had to smile or laugh. She made you happy. Rick noticed how he felt every time she walked by. He couldn't look at her without smiling, and it was impossible to have a negative thought when she was near.

The clown concept is simple: clowns make you happy. Seeing or thinking about them alters your mood in a positive way. Can you see where this might have its place in business? An organization wearing the figurative costume of a clown takes us off guard. It allows us to express ourselves in an alternative way, without the bonds of inhibition. The Clown Concept reduces the shields of protective armor that we use in business which keep us from showing our human side. The power of the clown breaks down the barriers of conflict, prejudice, and mistrust. What parts of your business could be improved by associating with happy icons?

We are not telling you to go out and buy a clown suit or make-up before giving your next presentation to a new client. We are saying that when barriers are broken down and honest negotiations occur, true win/win situations are more prevalent in any successful business relationship. The new client might even get to like you, and the scales can happily be tipped in your favor. Something as simple as a laugh, a smile, or the figurative wearing of the robes of the clown can be as powerful as a stack of computer reports and rational reasons to buy. We don't live in a rational world and we don't deal with rational people. It's emotions that move decisions. The next time negotiations, sales situations, or even internal conflicts get a little tense, think about the clown. It might just be your edge to a more profitable relationship.

RECAP:

- How do you feel when you see a clown?
- What does your face look like? Are you smiling?
- Clowns trigger positive emotions. Where could your company utilize these effects?
- Don't try to understand how it works, just use it!
- Does your company associate itself with laughter?
- Why was Ronald McDonald such a good idea?
- How can your company wear the figurative robes of a clown while maintaining its professional image?

Ideas this gives you for your business:

_____

_____

_____

_____

_____

_____

_____

CHAPTER 7

When You Humorize, You Humanize

Business is about human nature

"Humanizing is touching our feelings.
Humorizing is merely the vehicle to get there."

– Rick Segel

This is the essence of the entire book. No one wants to deal with people who are aloof, arrogant, cocky, or stuck up, or with those folks who sincerely believe their waste has no aroma. You know the type. The office know-it-all. The first one in the neighborhood to have a new sports car, people who walk with an air about them; as if you are inferior and they are superior. Don't we just hate these people? These are the ones who buy their clothes from the "Conspicuous Consumption Catalog Factory Outlet Store." We are *never* like that. Like the woman who complains that she's overweight but is only a size 5.

You don't like them. No one does, and they can lose sales and alienate potential buyers. Sure, sometimes they make a sale, but at what expense? Did they win the battle yet lose the war? Most likely the customer who deals with this type of individual won't come back and will usually tell some friends. People buy from—and build long-term relationships with—approachable people.

As much as we dislike the arrogant type of person, we are obligated to write this chapter for them. When you "humorize" a situation you humanize it, and the arrogant of the world need to humorize more than everyone else.

The concept of humorizing is simply putting a humorous twist on any situation. It's the same as politicians putting their spin on any situation or the way businesspeople capitalize on their advantages. If a small business is competing with a large one, the small businesspeople spin the facts and use all their advantages. A good example of a competitive spin is, "We are still small enough to know ya." The big store might have a larger assortment, but the small store buys for the individual needs of its customer.

The "humor twist" is taking a serious moment and breaking the mood or feeling and change a person or the person's behavior by derailing the train of thought. An example of the humor twist is two people seriously discussing any topic and someone's throwing in a question that has no bearing on the topic. It's a classic non sequitur. It's when someone asks, "How 'bout them Red Sox?"

A number of years ago when Rick was an active downtown woman's apparel retailer, he was at the midway point of the major sales event of the year: the infamous "sidewalk sale," when tensions were mounting over whether or not to mark down a rack of dresses. It was a hot day in the middle of July. Rick worked with his mother, a crusty old retailer who hated to mark down any merchandise. Rick argued in favor of marking it down and Ruth said, "No, NO, absolutely NOT!" The tension rose with the blood pressure. Neither side was giving in. Right in the middle of this heated discussion a big black dog came by, lifted its leg, and proceeded to pee on the goods. When that happens, all you can do is laugh. The dog had more power over the situation by humorizing it. Instantly Rick and Ruth each became human again. The dresses did get marked down, but much more than Rick would have liked. (They now call it the Fire Hydrant Sale.) The only difference between that event and you is that you will know when you are *intentionally* humorizing a situation. A few months ago Rick went for his annual physical. He goes to the Lahey Clinic, a typical mega-healthcare clinic. They call your name and send you to a small examining room. The nurse hands you a hospital gown that doesn't even come close to wrapping around anyone, let alone Rick. Rick strips down to his shoes, underpants, and the hospital gown that doesn't fit, and then he waits. Well, if someone is going to put Rick in a cubical unattended forever with nothing to occupy his mind, watch out! He has to be busy (he's an adult with the attention span of a two-year-old). So Rick goes through the drawers and finds scalpels, tape, rubber gloves, and assorted stuff that he has no idea how to use. Rick proceeds to try on the rubber gloves. Remember, he is wearing underpants, dressy black shoes, and an undersized hospital gown. He puts on the gloves, and lo and behold, who walks in but the doctor. Rick has a female doctor, and on seeing him she barks, "WHY DO YOU HAVE RUBBER GLOVES ON?"

Rick had to humorize a tight situation. His response changed the mood instantaneously. He said, "Well, I knew you were going to be wearing rubber gloves and I thought it was a formal affair." She couldn't keep a straight face and told him to keep the rubber gloves. Rick successfully humorized the situation.

How can you change a mood with just a funny comment? How can you humorize your next meeting? Do you look at every situation and ask yourself, "How can I humorize it?" Are you judging your communications on a laughter meter? When you ask yourself if there is enough sell in the ad, do you also ask if there is enough humor in the ad? Isn't it the same thing?

Did you ever notice that some of the best laughs come at a wake or funeral? Why? Because for many, humor is nature's defense mechanism for handling grief. One of our best friends is a comedian named Dave Fitzgerald. Dave does many USO tours and has made many national television appearances. This summer Dave was diagnosed with cancer. Because of Dave's ability to humorize situations, he was able to get through serious cancer surgery in which his bladder was removed. By putting the Humor Twist on every step of the way, he not only was able to cope himself, but also made it very bearable for those close to him. This did not mean he didn't cry or have the fears and concerns everyone else faces with this situation. He felt the fear, and found the humor in it anyway.

If using humor can help conquer a life-threatening illness, then what relatively minor problems in your company can be helped with humor? Dave has now developed part of his routine around this traumatic part of his life. How powerful is his comedic message? After almost all of Dave's shows, someone invariably comes up to him and says, "I had cancer but could never talk about it. Thank you!" Once people in the medical field saw him perform, he became an instant success.

Remember, every situation can be humorized. Inevitably there will be situations you choose not to humorize, but the possibility is still there.

RECAP:

- Any situation can be humorized.

- You can choose not to use the created humor in some situations.

- People buy from people they like, and people like humor.

- Ask how can we make this fun?

- How can you use the "humor twist?"

Authors' note on the word "humorize." We think we made up this word. We are not sure, but since we couldn't find it in spell check it must be ours! If anyone out there knows of the true origins of this word please shut up and keep it to yourself. We don't want to know! We want this little bit of glory, and besides, Webster was our childhood hero. Yeah, right!

Ideas this gives you for your business:

_____

_____

_____

_____

_____

_____

_____

CHAPTER 8

Associate Your Association

Are you associated?

"Make it fun and they will come."

– Rick Segel

M ost association memberships are down. There are many reasons why, but we are not going to dissect the reasons why. We are not here to talk about the association newsletter, though we could. We are not here to discuss the dues or the people in power. We are here to ask if your meetings are fun. Are they? Some cynics are saying, "We belong to our associations to get work and exchange ideas in a non-competitive manner." Okay, but we are talking about the way the ideas are being communicated and the overall attitude and environment of the association.

Associations are formed to self-educate, share ideas, and network. Part of learning is hearing the lesson. If you are sleeping or find that your mind is elsewhere, not much learning is happening (not to mention how little is learned when people don't even show up). We love the guy who fights against adding humor to a program and is then caught sleeping during a boring workshop. He always uses the excuse that the convention was so busy he didn't get enough sleep. Yeah, right! That is pure poppycock! The messenger was BORING!

When a program has humor, people stay awake. When a program is alive and exchanges ideas and information, there is usually humor present. It's the same as having a bowl of corn flakes without a sprinkle of sweetener. (Rick prefers Equal; Darren likes the real thing.) We would rather not have the cereal than eat it without the sweetener.

Why should any of your attendees travel to the land of the bland when our Yellow Brick Road of humor accomplishes more learning, more networking (as in everyone turning to their laughing neighbors and asking, "What did she say?'), and greater camaraderie by having the words covered with laughter. Remember Mary Poppins—"It takes a spoonful of sugar to make the medicine go down." She was talking about a meeting of the Civil Engineering Society of London.

Are your members enjoying their meetings? Are they smiling at the meetings? Or do they all look like they are going to die from terminal seriousness? ARE THEY THROWING AWAY YOUR NEWSLETTERS UNREAD? Do YOU enjoy attending? Do you go because you want to or because you feel obligated? Make it your field of fun. Build a fun association and they will come!

Darren and Rick hate these goody-two-shoes types, the rah-rah types who make you feel that joining the association is the same as hitting the beach at Normandy together. It is forced camaraderie. It's phony! Humor allows natural bonding without all the hullabaloo. We are into natural, as the rest of the world is. Don't give us polyester when we can have 100 percent pure cotton.

How do you do it? By first asking the question, "How can we make our association, its meetings, and our being members more fun?" It starts off that simple. You must let members go off on tangents about their attitude for fun. Encourage the wise guys. You want them involved. They are the ones who will give you that off-the-wall advice that they think is funny but everyone else thinks is crazy, which, when modified, becomes a workable suggestion. You want to get out of your box. You don't want to do the same old things.

Kiss a contrarian—they'll get you talking! Negativity is what people think about. Sorry if we burst somebody's bubble, but the news is negative. Watch *Apollo 13*. No one cared about that flight until it got into trouble. All we are suggesting is that it is a starting point. A common denominator to a positive path. Plus, if you get the negative types involved, they then become your allies.

Excitement builds on excitement, laughter builds on laughter, and the members and money keep on flowing into rather than out of your association. Somewhere in the middle of all this, learning occurs. We were having so much fun we forgot about that. This is what the *Laugh & Get Rich* philosophy is all about: the utilization of humor for a profitable result.

RECAP:

- Increase the fun, increase the membership.

- Humor creates a natural camaraderie.

- Make the newsletter fun and more will read it.

- Negatives are a common denominator. Use them to your advantage. How?

- Include the wise guys; they have the best ideas (when modified) and you make them your allies.

- Ask, "How can we make it more fun?" or "How can we add humor with positive learning?"

- Don't separate the fun from the learning.

- Members who enjoy membership are better recruiters.

- Do your members enjoy membership?

- Could you increase membership if things weren't so boring?

- How could humor aid in networking?

Ideas this gives you for your business:

_____

_____

_____

_____

_____

_____

_____

PART II

WHY IN BUSINESS?

CHAPTER 9

Positive Humor
vs. Negative

Who's the victim?

"The power of humor is like a magnet:
positive attracts, negative repels.
Use it wisely."

– Darren LaCroix

As we wrote the previous chapters we were laughing and giggling about things we couldn't and wouldn't write in this book. We had more fun at the expense of the differences among people. Yes, we made fun of people because they were different. We all know the classic stereotype groups: Jewish, African American, Polish American, Italian, fat people, skinny people, women, men, old people, stupid people, Southerners, Northerners, Yankees, large-chested women, Chicago Bears fans, policemen, retailers, fast food workers, and on and on.

Are some of these categories funny to us? Yes. Would it be funny to others? Sure. Would it be funny to everyone? NO! Not everything one does or says is funny. The point we are making is that negative humor hurts. Someone will always be offended. Offended employees are thinking more about being offended than they are about being productive. This impacts your bottom line. This kind of humor is just another form of harassment, and most harassment starts with an offensive joke. Think about what goes through someone's brain after being offended at work. "I don't deserve this crap!" "What am I doing here?" "Take this job and shove it!"

Now think about how much it would cost to replace this person. How much would it cost to fight a lawsuit? Or, if the employee puts up with it, what is the cost in lost productivity from that individual? What about the other employees who will get caught in the middle? How much will productivity be hurt by that?

Let's reframe your thinking. Negative humor is an expense. IT COSTS MONEY! We are not here to discuss what is politically correct or isn't. Who cares? Those people don't have a life anyway! We are here to talk about making money with humor, and negative humor can be a dangerous and unnecessary risk.

Did you get what we just did? Please say yes! Darren didn't, but what do you expect from a guy like him? *Now* do you get it, or are you just too dumb?

How do you feel right now? First, Rick insulted politically correct people, and then both of us insulted *you*. Do you want to read on? Even an apology from us won't really help, but we did this for your own good (don't you love it when people say that to you?). How many times do you think such insults happen in corporate America, and how do you think it affects productivity? Eliminate expressions like "those people," and never put someone down, as it only alienates the person and creates a negative effect on the work environment.

We can hear the groans now. What *can* we laugh about? Nothing!!

THE END

Only kidding! Who got offended? No one did. There are plenty of things we can laugh about without having to put people down. You can laugh at the behavior but not the person or group of people. Laugh about issues and frustrations rather than people. An example from the retail world is the type of customer we all deal with, whom Rick likes to call "the Assassin." In comedy they're called hecklers, but their motivation is usually alcohol. The Assassin is the friend or associate of the customer. The customer is ready to say yes when the Assassin walks in and says, "Are you sure you can't do any better?" or "We have a lot of other places to look." Who needs them?

Note that in joking about the Assassin, our humor is directed towards the action, not the person. It doesn't matter what gender or race the person is, or even their hair color. It isn't even part of the story. The actions of people can open the door to positive, non-offensive laughter and humor.

Dr. Norman Vincent Peale wrote about the power of positive thinking, a concept that holds true in humor as well. Somewhere along the way negative humor crept into mainstream thinking and has been causing problems ever since. There are just as many positive things to laugh about if we merely look for them. Positive humor is the invisible asset on the balance sheet.

RECAP:

- Can you see how picking on someone or on a group can reverse the benefits of humor?

- How does offensive humor create negative self-talk?

- Does negative humor cost money?

- How can you use the invisible asset of positive humor?

Ideas this gives you for your business:

_____

_____

_____

_____

_____

_____

_____

_____

_____

_____

_____

CHAPTER 10

Humor Goes Both Ways

The pay's not great, but it's fun!

"Employees who have fun at work are
willing to go home with less money in pocket."

– Confucius and/or Darren and Rick

Yes, we all like to do business with people who are having fun; we buy from them and many times we buy more. Sometimes we say the service was pleasant or upbeat, or we say, "What a nice person." Those comments are a result of the use of some type of humor or playful behavior. So, yes, humor increases sales. But it also has another effect. Both sides of the balance sheet are affected by humor. It is as important to reduce costs as it is to increase sales. Humor can reduce turnover because people want to work at a place that is fun. You can even get people to work for nothing when the fun is strong enough.

Last summer, Rick's daughter worked as an intern for a Top-40 radio station. She was paid nothing for the opportunity to work there. She loved it so much she wanted to go back this summer. Rick said, "No, get a real job." (He was tired of supporting her.) As we write this, his other daughter is working as an intern in

Hilton Head, South Carolina. She works the second shift, 45 hours a week, including weekends. Her employers do pay for a place to live, but she must pay for her own food. For this wonderful opportunity she receives the King's ransom of $150.00 *a month.* She wouldn't trade it for all the money in the world. Would you take a pay cut for the opportunity to work in a job that was so much fun you couldn't wait to get to work Monday mornings?

We believe that many of us would trade in the materialistic trappings for a truly fun existence. But why would you want to when you can have it all? You can have fun and make money at the same time. Just knowing that you can get employees to work for you for next to nothing is a fun thought for any entrepreneur. It really is more than that crude bit of capitalism creeping through. It is living an attitude of fun while making a significant contribution to the well-being of our economic society. It sounds so good you feel as if you are doing something wrong. You are not. You are applying the *Laugh & Get Rich* philosophy.

RECAP:

- Could you hire people to work for next to nothing because it's such a fun place?
- How could you make your business a fun place to work?
- What are the key elements for a fun place for employees?
- Do you think internal humor is as important as external humor?

Ideas this gives you for your business:

_____

_____

_____

_____

_____

_____

_____

_____

_____

_____

_____

CHAPTER 11

The Funsuckers

There's one in every office.
Who is yours?

"Some people bring happiness wherever
they go, some people whenever they go."

– Oscar Wilde

Yes, Virginia, there is a Funsucker! This is not a myth. It exists (though often in disguise). The soul of a Funsucker can possess a co-worker's body temporarily. These creatures say they want to have fun but they really want to sabotage the lives of the true "fun" seekers. You know the type. They say things like "that's not funny" or "grow up and act your age."

They suck the life out of any situation by sucking the humor out of it. You know the sponges that can dampen even a New Year's Eve celebration. You are in your office laughing and joking, brainstorming and coming up with silly ideas. They walk into the room and simply turn their noses up, roll their eyes, and give you that tsk, tsk look. Everyone's posture in the room changes. (Every office has one; it's mandatory. It was a law passed by Congress in 1832).

You really want to slap these people silly, but in today's society you just can't do that. Unfortunately, even Funsuckers have rights, though we are looking into changing that.

The worst thing is that these Funsuckers have an innate power to stifle creativity as much as a 110-degree humid day stifles the way you feel. How valuable was the idea you never got to? All because the Funsucker showed up. These are the people who complain there weren't enough red M&M's in their bag of M&M's. These are the people who think the chicken dance is worthless. Don't feel bad if you think it's dumb. So do we! But it's meant to be dumb. The Funsucker breed thinks that 4th of July fireworks are noise pollution. These people think Robin Williams can't keep his train of thought, that Billy Crystal is too ethnic, that Steven Wright should go to a self-esteem workshop, and Bob Hope is a communist. Get the picture?

Funsuckers really *suck* (the life out of any situation). We know you think this expression is a little strong coming from the two founders of the Humor Institute, but it's true. The sooner we are able to identify the Funsucker, the better we are able to learn how to deal with these serpents of life. Remember, these people complain that things are going to be bad, and every time something bad happens they can say, "I told you so!" It is their own self-fulfilling prophecy. They get their kicks out of destroying things. They get a rise out of bringing things down.

How do you deal with them? Easy! First, recognize them for who they are. Second, tell them that they are Funsuckers. That really scores big points with them. Then, maybe they will avoid you. Third, avoid them (run away and hide if you must). Then, buy a copy of this book for them or give them your copy. They will start to get the point.

Let's get serious for a minute. If you have Funsuckers in your organization, they are affecting the bottom line and will gradually become a liability through their chipping away at the morale of your greatest resource, your people. When you stifle creativity (a direct by-product of humor), you cost everyone in the company the opportunity for added growth. Look at your pay stub; a fun-sucked environment is an invisible deduction from everyone's pay. When someone sucks the fun out of a project, they are limiting the full potential of that project.

The reason we can make that statement is because if creativity is a direct link to humor or laughter, then curtailing humor is curtailing the level of creativity. Notice we said level. There will be some doubting Thomases out there who believe that humor has no effect on creativity. To them we say, "Enjoy the dream while it lasts." Remember our adage, "People who think funny are thinking." How many companies today suffer from employees who just don't think?

Employees often do things by rote; they are asked to do the same or similar functions over and over again, always in the same way. How many times have we heard the excuse, "Well, that's the way we've always done it?" The employee runs the risk of losing a good customer for you because they have become operationally focused and not customer-focused. Look at laughter and humor as the fun and easy gateway to creativity, the open door. The Funsucker simply shuts the door and forces creativity to be sought in more difficult ways—as in breaking down the front door, picking the lock, or breaking a window to get inside. Humor is an easier way of getting inside creativity. In the end we're not as tired because we didn't have to work as hard to get in. How many times have we all said, "Today was a fun day at work"? Probably not enough, and usually when we can't say it, it is because of some Funsucker. Eliminate the Funsucker and let the creative juices flow.

People no longer stay in places or at jobs that aren't fun. The days of being chained to one company are over. People are willing to sacrifice money for environment, and we, as companies, can no longer afford to employ Funsuckers.

Ask someone who works at your company if they like working there. What do you think they will say? What would they answer if their best friend asked the same question? Let's define "like" for a second. "Like" is having a comfortable atmosphere in which to work. You can have a company with great benefits and great pay, but if the Funsucker works in your department, all the good can be wiped out practically instantaneously because they have no time for a little fun or playful behavior. If this person has contact with other parts of your company, he or she can become a deadly cancer, slowly and quietly eating away at the very fiber of any organization. No one is immune.

What thoughts do you think go through people's heads when they have to deal with the Funsucker at any level? If you don't see any Funsuckers in your company, make sure you look in the mirror, too. Chances are, however, that since you bought this book you are already humor-inclined. If you were given this book, take notice. You might just be a member of The Funsucker Society of America (FSA).

Make a sign at work with the word Funsucker encircled by the international sign for NO. It just might do the trick and get the Funsuckers laughing. It will also help those with Funsucker tendencies to stop before gaining full-fledged membership in the FSA. They will start to get the message. Usually all it takes is shifting their point of view to make them converts to the *Laugh & Get Rich* philosophy. The sad truth is that we have never been trained to be able to use humor effectively at work and therefore think that it doesn't belong in that environment. WRONG! Go forth and laugh.

RECAP:

- Funsuckers are real. They exist and must be handled as any other business challenge.
- Try not to have them in the first place.
- They directly impact your turnover rate.
- They limit creativity.
- Are your people operationally-focused or customer-focused?
- Funsuckers reduce the problem-solving ability of both individuals and groups.
- Who are your Funsuckers? Why? What can you do about them?
- Make the sign...others in the office will enjoy it, too.
- Avoid Funsuckers whenever possible.
- They SUCK...bottom line profits invisibly.

Ideas this gives you for your business:

_____

_____

_____

_____

_____

_____

_____

_____

CHAPTER 12

Life and Death Humor

From the CEO of Laughter

"Laughter filters down from the top."

– Rick Segel

The very best example of a company that blends the benefit of humor for both sales and morale is the much-talked-about Southwest Airlines. It all starts with someone at the top, and at the top of Southwest is Herb Kelleher, the grand pooh-bah of humor. Kelleher is a cross between a genius and a registered tooty-fruity. He believes in having fun and shows it. His welcoming video to new employees shows him with his key executives singing a rap song. He encourages his pilots and flight attendants to have fun and use the tool of humor.

All of us have heard the stories about Southwest Airlines, so the one company we didn't want to use as an example was Southwest. However, Rick recently took a Southwest flight from Los Angeles to San Jose. What follows is the actual safety instruction announcement made by the senior flight attendant. Once we heard this we had to include it in this book. It went exactly like this.

Please take the instruction card out of the pocket in front of you. You know, in the pocket where you usually throw your gum wrappers. Now, please place the seat belt around your lips...I mean your hips. This will be a no choking...I mean, a no smoking flight. But, if you would like to have a cigarette, please feel free to go out on the patio area where we will be showing the movie *Gone With the Wind.* If you are traveling with a small child (or with someone who acts like one) and the oxygen masks drop down, IF they have been good, put it on them. If not, the heck with them. The oxygen will cost $2.00 the first minute and $1.00 thereafter.

Upon landing she continued with:

As soon as our wonders of aviation get to the gate, you can get off of this tub but, while you are waiting, please sign up for our frequent flyer program. It's not as good as being married to a flight attendant or pilot, but it's the next best thing!

What made the whole experience so interesting was watching the other passengers. They were listening, really listening. Take any flight from any other airline and watch the passengers read the paper, listen to their Walkmans, or fall asleep during the safety lecture. This is a life and death announcement, yet people listen only when the message is delivered with humor. It's almost a little scary. We take a lot of flights and no one ever listens to the announcements. Is this so dumb to communicate in a way that makes people want to listen to what you say? To think you might be able to say it in even fewer words!

The old line from the National Speakers Association is, "a professional speaker doesn't have to make people laugh, unless you want to get paid." What this means is that people will and do pay to be entertained. Even the best material in the world is not digested in the way you intend it to be if not presented in a fun, easy-to-understand manner. How often do you read meeting minutes thoroughly? Has anyone in your department not done what they were supposed to do because they didn't read the minutes or the boring memo? Do these mistakes cost money and time? Of course they do.

Why not *humunicate?* "Humunicate" means to communicate with humor! If a manager's goal is to communicate information to subordinates, it only makes sense to communicate in a manner that is easy to understand, is easy to remember, and captures one's undivided attention. That makes sense!!

Southwest joked about one of the most important parts of their job which is making their customers aware of the safety features of the aircraft and what to do in the case of an emergency. These were instructions that can save lives. How much more important can you get? In the event of an actual emergency, you don't get the chance to recap or ask the flight attendant "What did you say?" The Southwest attendants made you remember by grabbing your attention, forcing you to listen not by threatening you, but by making it fun. It was non-offensive (well if you were a smoker you might have been a little miffed), but for the rest of the passengers it was good, clean fun.

Rick is a Gold Medallion frequent flyer on Delta Airlines, and he can't recite even one line from the flight attendant's message. Delta is one of the most professional airlines in the industry. The pilots and flight attendants look and act like bankers. They exude an air of professionalism on every flight, but they have fallen short in truly communicating their message. Sure, they say all the right things, but it just isn't as effective. People like to have fun and play games. All Southwest really did was take a situation and humorize it. Think of all the boring repetitive jobs you have at your company or organization. Think about the interactions you have with the people who pay your bills—the customers. Ask yourself, "How can I humorize all of those tasks?"

Darren and Rick say, "There is humor in everything we do— you just gotta find it!"

Southwest also encourages its flight attendants to get dressed up in costumes during different holidays. You know, the Easter Bunny at Easter and various costumes at Halloween. The employees love the feeling this gives them. They feel as if they aren't even working. It relaxes the customer and puts the customer in the right frame of mind. The real bonus to Southwest is that they used to pay their employees less than the rest of the industry but their turnover rate is almost non-existent. Some of their locations can take up to 5 years to get transferred to. In 1998, during a tight employment market, Southwest had approximately 4,200 openings and more than 80,000 people applying for those jobs. This is sound business and good humor.

Customers want to do business with fun, upbeat, positive people who can laugh at themselves. That is not any different than what employees want. Why managers still frown upon the use of humor and believe that getting serious is good for business is beyond us. It is BAD business and shows a lack of creativity and commitment to alternative ways of succeeding. The paradigm is shifting, the bandwagon is gaining momentum, the train is leaving the station, and the fat lady is singing. Yogi Berra said it's over, the curtain is being pulled, the battle lines are drawn, and the clichés are finished. The corporate world is finally starting down our Yellow Brick Road. They will find the great Humor Oz at the end of the road, and your organization will thrive and survive in your Emerald City of fun and profits. But, ease on down the road.

P.S. In the year since we wrote this chapter, Rick has had another Southwest experience that is worth stopping the presses for. Rick took a crowded Southwest flight from Chicago to Manchester, New Hampshire. Only this time there was no laughter, playful behavior, fun announcements, or even the attitude of fun. It was terrible. Rick felt like a cow on a boxcar to the slaughter. Remove the fun and Southwest is just another pack 'em in, get 'em out quick, budget carrier. The fun set them apart. The fun can set you apart as well.

RECAP:

- It takes acceptance by upper management. It takes a friend at the top like Herb Kelleher to make a difference. Can you make a difference?

- Even the most mundane things can be humorized. What mundane things do you have that need a shot of humor?

- Customers love to laugh and humor gets attention. How could you have your customers laughing?

- Employees love it and want to work for you for more than just money.

- Humor sharpens listening skills.

- Humor can be used to get attention. Without attention there is no communication and communication is what we are after.

Ideas this gives you for your business:

_____

_____

_____

_____

_____

_____

_____

CHAPTER 13

To Be Written

The fruit is in the fruition

"If it's fun…it gets done!"

– Darren LaCroix

How many great ideas have you had? How many did you follow through on? How many projects, at work and at home, have been started but never completed? Have you ever thought of writing your own book? Why haven't you? Whether it's work or personal, we all have so much going on and so little extra time to do the things we would like to do that many of our brilliant ideas die in their tracks without us! We have to bring them to life. Many times we think, "What a great idea!" The next thought to follow is, "But it's a lot of work," or "Man, that's going to suck!" Immediately, the sickle of Death has slashed your ideas.

What if the work was fun? Your idea or task would be much more likely to come to fruition. Ask the question, "How can this be made fun?" Volunteer organizations have already figured this out. How else could they get people to do monotonous or difficult work for free? The good of the cause is important, too, but the best and most successful organizations utilize fun to the max.

Rick and Darren kept writing because when they were together they had so much fun. This book came to life because of a passion for the subject and for having fun. How do you get children to do things they would find boring? Make it fun! Remember flying food? Adults are just big kids who have been conditioned by the business world to think that they cannot have fun as they work. It's time to teach and re-teach professionals that fun motivates!

RECAP:

- An idea or a task is more likely to happen and be done right if the process is fun.

- What ideas in your business or personal life have you not followed through on? How could you make their completion fun enough to get started?

Ideas this gives you for your business:

CHAPTER 14

The Poppins Principle

Humor-based training –
the spoonful of sugar

---

*"Just a spoonful of sugar
makes the medicine go down."*

– Mary Poppins

D arren was hired to humorize a training video for one of the largest franchise companies in the United States. He was absolutely shocked to find out that this was the company's first attempt at using humor in training videos. The irony was that this franchise had one of the longest running advertising campaigns in history that used humor! They believed in selling with humor, but never utilized humor for training its franchisees and their employees. It's the old goose and gander thing...the dreaded double standard. This must cease!

Why is it that when people think about training, they instantly think about it like it's something they have to do? Like going to your distant relative's graduation ceremony. You don't want to go, you don't like being there, and you know it's going to be BORING. You can name at least 10 other places you would rather be. However, we all have relatives we like and want to be with, and usually the single common denominator is fun. Yes, fun. We want to be with some people because they are fun. This is as natural an instinct as there is. It is the spoonful of sugar. You don't want to be at the graduation but at least cousin Susie will be there and she's a lot of fun.

If the concept of the spoonful of sugar makes social situations more bearable, a spoonful of humor will make training more enjoyable. Serious trainers who are reading this are saying, "We play games, isn't that enough?" Well, what we are suggesting is the concept of humor-based training, which, simply put, means placing the ribbon of humor throughout all of the training. The humor needs to be as important as the content; you must embody "laugh-while-you-learn training."

In the words of the great trainer's trainer Bob Pike, "Learning is directly proportional to the amount of fun you have." We believe in going one step beyond fun to laughter, belly laughs, snorts, giggles, and snickers. Too many trainers believe that if they just play a game it will cover the need for fun. We don't buy into that concept. Your goal is to have enjoyable training that is remembered and used. You want your participants to leave saying, "That was fun," and to have a grasp of what was being communicated, not saying "Why did we play that game?"

Humor and fun must be strategically used to drive home the point without anyone's realizing they have been humorized. The trainer should strive to make a seamless connection between the important information given and the degree of humor used. You cannot make a delineation between the learning and the fun; it's the marriage of the two that creates an atmosphere of optimal effectiveness. In this way the information is copied on the hard disc of the brain almost effortlessly, just like pushing the save keys on your computer.

Why does that happen? Because humor is the most obvious thing that we, as trainers, sometimes forget. With humor-based training we are delivering information with its own built-in memory peg. Laughter is that memory peg, and when we associate it with our information the likelihood of retention is greatly increased. It is as if we are saying, "Here is the point and here is the how and why you should remember it."

Most people, when asked out of the blue to tell a joke, can't remember any. However, if someone tells a joke, suddenly everyone remembers a half dozen they want to share. What humor does is create an enjoyable filing system for the mind. For those of you who don't have files any more, humor also works like a Web browser, pointing the way to the information stored in our very own brain Internets.

Humor creates the anchor for learning. How many great speakers have you ever heard who didn't use humor? Humor is more than placing a printed circuit board with a directory into the brain; it can divert the power to stimulate the brain. We are not suggesting that you have to be mindless to receive information, but humor relaxes the brain the same way hypnosis does. A hypnotist always relaxes the subject first (you don't want to put your audience to sleep). Then, when the subject is in a totally relaxed state, the hypnotist makes suggestions that work. Hypnosis works on the basic principle that in a relaxed state, suggestions will reach the subconscious mind. Laughter is perhaps another way of relaxing the person and the mind, and frees or distracts someone from the day-to-day stressors of life.

The zip-locked mind is the same as the zip-locked bag, nothing gets in or out. No fresh air and no ideas. We all read body language. Especially trainers. We can tell when the attendees are with us or not. Too many times we see the audience wearing down, and as a quick fix we throw in a funny story. Though it does work, humor is more effective as a tool than a crutch. Start off on a high plane and keep the laughter level consistent on that high plane.

It is easier for a humorist to be a trainer than it is for a trainer be a humorist. Why? Because the humorist is more skilled and practiced at making points wrapped with humor. For trainers who find this new, don't feel bad. Just implement humor and this concept will become another weapon in your arsenal of training tools.

Training is like anything else. It's not what you do but how you do it. If a trainer has a boring, flat monotone or an expressionless delivery, the best game from *Games Trainers Play* might help a little but it will not have the impact that the full concept of humor-based training can have. Get out of the boring-fun-boring scenario and work to weave the ribbon of fun throughout your programs. From the clothes you wear, to the way you speak, to the props you use, humor-based training is the total enlightened training experience that is the marriage of learning and laughter.

(May they live happily ever after!)

RECAP:

- Fun and laughter are the spoonful of sugar for any personal interaction, especially training.

- It must be a total commitment to the use of humor—placing its value on an even par with the content.

- Humor-based training—just do it!

- It is more than a joke when the audience gets sleepy. It is the well-planned humor resting spots.

- Humor is an emotional memory peg.

Ideas this gives you for your business:

_____

_____

_____

_____

_____

_____

_____

_____

_____

CHAPTER 15

Our Government Invests in Humor?

Why don't you?

> *"Unhappy employees + more money =*
> *rich, unhappy employees."*
>
> – Alan Weiss, Ph.D.
> Author of *Million Dollar Consulting*

December 13, 1995, on the front page of *The Wall Street Journal*, above the fold, was an article titled, "When Democrats Need to Lighten up, He Has Laugh Lines." The article talks about a colleague of ours (we don't know him but he is still a colleague) who is a humor consultant to the White House. He writes jokes for the Clintons and Al Gore (apparently Mrs. Gore doesn't need any help). Think about it, our tax money is being spent on a humor consultant. Do those Democrats know something you should know?

It's not just Democrats; the Republicans have a humor consultant as well. You would think Congress and Rush Limbaugh would be enough of a joke, but no. We are paying tax money to a man named Mark Katz to write one-liners at the rate of $500.00 for a few lines or the deluxe humorous speech at $7,000.00.

Is this government waste or is it government wisdom? From our humble point of view they are right on the money (literally). What good are the greatest ideas, thoughts, concepts, or laws if they can't be presented in a manner that is digestible, keeps the audience's attention, and aids their memories? Those folks in Washington aren't dumb all the time. The most important thing for any political figure to be is "one of the people." They all say that. There is no better way to be part of the people than to use humor.

Remember what we said earlier: "When you humorize you humanize." This is about as important to a politician as your relationships are to you. Not only your relationships with your customer base, but those with your co-workers and your employees. People want to be associated with nice people, real people, fun people, and the proverbial "NICE GUY." We describe people by saying, "What a nice person." Why? Maybe it's only because of a funny line or the lighthearted approach to life which they have.

Humor is that direct line to being liked, accepted, and trusted. Mark Katz would have done wonders for Nixon. Dick might not have had to resign. Katz has done wonders for Vice President Al Gore, Mr. Excitement himself. He had a stiff, boring image. *The Wall Street Journal* noted, "He's so boring that his Secret Service code name is Al Gore," so in an effort to change this image, "Mr. Gore had himself wheeled in a hand truck at one affair (as if he was a statue) and launched into self-deprecating humor." That was the last thing anyone would have expected this old family politician to have done. It worked. Now he is referred to as "Al Gore, bore no more," according to the *Washington Post.*

How does this apply to your company? Can you change your image by the use of some humor? If your first response is "I don't think so," then you will get the best laughs and the most mileage out of humor. The reason: no one will be expecting it. One of the best ways to invoke laughter is by doing the unexpected! We always get a laugh out of the meeting planners who frown on the use of humorists at a meeting. Especially when they say we don't want "that type" at our meetings. Then they go on to say, "This is serious business."

What could be more serious than the Presidency? *The Wall Street Journal* article quotes Paul Begala, the Republican humor consultant, as saying, "Too many liberals have had their funny bones removed." Does that sound like your company? Wake up! This stuff works to get to the same end results that you are reaching for. Only you are having fun along the way.

The concept of the marriage between humor and business is difficult to accept because of the mindset we were brought up with. The two don't mix at first glance. It's the same as mixed marriages, be they a mix of religious, racial, or social differences. It's time to change conventional wisdom. No more humor bigots!

Mark Katz's mother summed it up well in her response to a compliment about her son from President Clinton: "You know, you just complimented Mark for the same things I used to spank him for." Many of us still believe that the use of humor is a taboo. It's not.

We hope that this book helps others believe in and tap into the power of humor. The same way a Vermont Rabbi turned stand-up comic because he believed that if the congregation was laughing he would know it was a spiritual experience. If you can harness the power of humor you will be loved, respected, listened to, and—most important (that's why we keep on saying it)—remembered.

When the front line manager holds these qualities it always goes much further with employees than any other form of motivation. The best example of this took place when Rick had a meeting with his employees at Ruth's to make the announcement that Margie, his wife, was leaving to work full-time with Rick on his speaking and writing career. She had worked at Ruth's for 24 years and was an integral part of every major decision of the business. All the employees were upset that she was going to leave until Rick read the description of the type of person who was needed to replace her. The first thing he read was that the person had to have a good sense of humor and know how to have fun at work while getting things moving forward. The faces of the employees changed immediately. Their fear had been of a new boss who was going to be hard-nosed and tough.

You can be tough and have a sense of humor. It just works better to be both. Being tough is not devoid of laughter or fun. You can still maintain the highest of standards with a smile on your face and the occasional laugh to let people know you are human and approachable. It is easier to maintain standards with communication than without, and humor is part of the vehicle of communications.

RECAP:

- The government finally did something right.
- Humor works in a place you would least expect it.
- Between *The Wall Street Journal* and the White House, humor is gaining new respectability and credibility.
- It's now time for you to lighten up your image for added productivity.
- This chapter is a "why not you," not a "how to." How-to comes later.
- Self-deprecating humor does not diminish your effectiveness as a leader.
- The more you relate to your front line, the better the line of communication and the more open employees are to your ideas, concepts, and leadership.

Ideas this gives you for your business:

_____

_____

_____

_____

_____

_____

_____

_____

CHAPTER 16

Sex is Dead! (Did That Get Your Attention?)

Sell to the Boomer, do it with humor

"Different…is being different."

– Rick Segel

N o, of course sex isn't dead. This chapter has two purposes. First, to demonstrate the shock value of a catchy title, which of course tweaked your interest in reading this chapter. Second, to say that sex isn't what it used to be.

We live in a society in which instant gratification isn't quick enough. We get only a nanosecond to grab your interest and only 7 or 8 minutes, at best, before you are ready for a commercial break. Traditional ways of grabbing and maintaining interest just don't work any more. We are of the belief that they never really worked to begin with, but forced ourselves to believe that tradition was the only way to go.

We were wrong! Absolutely wrong! Dull and boring is dull and boring. Shock radio works because we want DIFFERENT.

Humor is different because so many stuffed-shirt, by-the-book engineering types from the great corporations have told us that we should not use it. Thank you for making our job that much easier. These types have created a corporate culture that makes small amounts of humor go a long way. They have opened the door for a boon of freethinking, daring, playful entrepreneurs who are laughing all the way to the bank. Apple's relaxed, laid-back policy on needless dress codes started a revolution that actually made the great giant IBM go with a dress-down day. Rick could never understand how wearing a three-piece suit helped in creativity. Most of his best ideas happen when he is either sitting on the john with his pants pulled down, in the shower with his clothes off, or in bed, and what he wears there is none of your business.

If creativity is the goal, and obviously it is, 'cause creativity pays the big bucks, then maybe IBM should have shower breaks in the middle of the day and encourage 20-minute dumps. If this sounds a bit too crude, good! You will remember it. If I had politely written "go to the rest room," you wouldn't remember this paragraph. No, I am not suggesting that blue, off-color, or vulgar humor will work. Absolutely not! What I am saying is that stretching the line of good taste without crossing it or breaking it can be another good source of humor.

Now, for all of you disappointed souls waiting for our essay on why sex is dead, here it comes. We couldn't let a good headline go to waste, since an attention-getting line is a terrible thing to waste. In the '60s, '70s, and '80s, sex was hot. It sold everything from soap to cars. It motivated the world. It motivated our behavior in almost every aspect of our lives. Rick grew up in the '60s when half the population of the United States was under 25. With youth you have active hormones. We were the Baby Boomer generation, the Woodstock people. (No, Darren wasn't there, but he could have been if his boss had let him have the time off.) We didn't trust the government because it told us killing Commies was cool. We dodged the draft and smoked funny-looking cigarettes. We preached to "tell it like it is."

Well, not only are we the generation now in power, but we are graying. We are fighting the aging process, kicking and punching all the way to the gym. All to no avail. We have accepted the varicose veins and the pants that need more room. And the dates we dreaded with the male or female who had a "great personality" but was not much to look at are somehow more appealing.

No, sex isn't dead, but there are some parts of our human anatomies that are succumbing to the will of Father Time. Fun is replacing the previous motivator of choice. Sex symbols aren't selling the products like they once did— real people are. Don't confuse the last statement to mean that celebrities aren't making endorsements. Sure they are, but they have to be human, approachable, and fun. Plastic people are going out faster than polyester at a sheep farm.

So how does that trend affect the generations that come after the Baby Boomers? The same way the Boomers were affected by the generation that preceded it, with one major exception. Generation X likes what we stood for. They like our music, à la *The Big Chill* and *Forrest Gump* soundtracks. They agree with many of our values. Mothers and daughters are wearing the same clothes, and Rick and his son wear/share the same shirts. I wouldn't be caught dead wearing anything my father would wear. In the '60s and '70s a clothing store was either Missy (old lady) or Junior (young and hip). The times they-are-a-changing. Humor sells, fun sells. In the '60s, the Beatles sang about a revolution. Well, grab your clown noses, put on your Groucho glasses, and get ready— the revolution has begun.

RECAP:

- Shock value has value.
- Sex isn't the motivator it once was, because of aging Baby Boomers.
- The times they-are-a-changing.
- Humor is replacing sex as the Number 1 motivator.
- We said this before but it is worth repeating: humor humanizes. We live in a society of real people who aren't impressed with anything phony (except Gucci watches).
- Clean fun has replaced dirty sex (sometimes).
- To sell to the Boomer...do it with humor.

Ideas this gives you for your business:

_____

_____

_____

_____

_____

_____

_____

_____

PART III

TOOLS TO USE

CHAPTER 17

The Cushioning Concept

How to cushion the situation

"If you can't do it well, learn to enjoy doing it badly."

– Unknown

The Cushioning Concept refers to many different aspects of our business lives that help to cushion tense or difficult situations. One of them involves giving praise to those people who are respected and highly regarded within your company or industry.

Did you ever receive a compliment so effusive or sticky-sweet that you lost respect for the person giving the compliment? The person giving the compliment means well. In most cases they are motivated by love, respect, or awe, as a 10-year-old is in awe of Michael Jordan. How does a person express sincere thanks and appreciation without sounding like a complete idiot or a starstruck little kid? This is the perfect situation for strategically placed laughter. This is what we refer to as the Cushioning Concept.

Both of us, Darren and Rick, have the highest respect and awe for one person: Alan Weiss, Ph.D. He is our idol, king, emperor, leader, mentor, guru, and all-around know-it-all. (It made us feel better just saying those things.) Alan Weiss is a past president of the New England Speakers Association. He has authored 5 books and receives fees for his work equivalent to the entire gross national product of some small developing countries. He is extremely bright, clever, creative, and funny. We feel honored and privileged to have worked with him. (Darren just yelled, "Aren't we going overboard?" No, we really believe this stuff.)

The setting for our story is Alan's final meeting as president of NESA. He was presenting his departing thoughts and advice to the membership and openly admitted that his future involvement would have to be limited due to time constraints. This was an emotional time for his disciples and followers. Darren did not want this moment to end without letting Alan know how much he had affected Darren's life and career. He wanted to get up at the end of Alan's presentation and tell Alan and the membership how he felt and that he, along with others, had nominated Alan for the Cavett Robert Award, the highest National Speakers Association award possible.

Here is how it happened. Darren got up after Alan spoke and made the announcement that he had nominated Alan. Then he threw in the line, "I know you are not going to get it...but we did nominate you anyway." With that the audience erupted with laughter. Why? The truth of the matter was that as much as Alan was admired locally, he had limited involvement nationally and did not have the exposure to warrant such an award. To our chapter, he was "The Godfather." Most admire him, even though at that point he had not been involved nationally and had never served on any national committee, been on the board, run any conventions, or done any of the other things one has to do to be considered. What Darren did was simply to say the things that were on the minds of many of the older members who knew Alan had given of himself to our chapter but just wasn't involved enough at the national level for this award.

An interesting side note was that the president-elect of the National Speakers Association was sitting beside me and gave the largest laugh of them all. Then he mumbled a statement that he, meaning Darren, was good. Why? Because instead of making himself look like a wide-eyed, innocent newcomer, he gained stature and respect for being able to laugh at himself while still showing respect for Alan. This is win/win humor. The best part is that the person Darren wanted to thank and impress, Alan, was more impressed with this tongue-in-cheek compliment than he would have been if it had been delivered as a sticky-sweet, I love you, butt-kissing, may-I-shine-your-shoes type of approach. He showed dignity, but made this demigod human. Humor humanized the situation.

What makes this a memorable situation and what can we learn? Can you think of any similar situations that you may have found yourself in where the use of humor would have made your task more effective? Do you sometimes want to give a compliment but don't want to sound like you are kissing up? Do you want to be enthusiastic, yet savvy? Humor is the best tool that can accomplish all of that in such a short time. In 10 seconds Darren accomplished what takes others years. This is a powerful tool to be utilized.

RECAP:

- Say what they are thinking.

- The more tense the situation the more valuable humor is.

- In sticky-sweet situations humor acts as a lubricant to make the point more believable.

- Without the humor the compliment giver can actually lose respect.

- Compliments become softer on the receiver. We all know situations in which a compliment goes on and on, and we don't know how to accept it.

- Many people don't take compliments well. People get embarrassed.

Ideas this gives you for your business:

_____

_____

_____

_____

_____

_____

_____

_____

_____

CHAPTER 18

Michelle's Rule

We do business with people we have fun with

"We do business with Michelle because we like to do business with people we have fun with."

– Rick Segel

That's profound! Who's Michelle? She must be from the Harvard Business School. Wrong! She is Rick's travel agent. So what? Why is he doing business with her? One day Rick's wife, Margie, asked, "Do you like the new travel agent?" Rick's reply was quick and to the point, "Yes, Michelle is a lot of fun to do business with!" Then he stopped and realized what he had said. He was doing business with someone because she was fun to do business with?

Please, before your mind starts to wander about what fun means, let me inform you that Rick is an experienced businessperson and business traveler and is not easily impressed. Rick has been running his own company for the past 27 years. He has been happily married for 30 years, and the type of fun you might be thinking about is really not a motivation to him. A sex symbol he is not.

You must be thinking there are other reasons for doing business with Michelle. It's not price. All travel agents have basically the same prices, and the type of travel Rick does is always pretty much at the same price. Is she convenient? No! Her office is 45 minutes away. There is no parking. And if you could find a place to park, you wouldn't feel safe leaving your car there. Is she efficient? Yes, but plenty of other travel agents are efficient.

So why is Rick booking around 100,000 yearly air miles, plus hotels rooms and car rentals, with Michelle? Because it is fun? Wait a minute, some great retailer or business tycoon must have figured this out. What do you get when you mix fun and business? It is called entertainment shopping or misdirected, soft-suggestive selling. This places the emphasis on fun first, the product second. The days of turning the customer upside down until all the money falls out are over! They were very good years but they are over.

Many businesses today have reached the pinnacle in quality, service, selection, and value. What else is there to compete over? Fun and humor, of course! What other tool can separate you from your competition and create a more loyal customer, a happier customer, and a more forgiving customer? Nothing! If you compete on price, you are merely a commodity. If you compete on selection, you are only as good as your last merchandise mix (and every buyer guesses wrong once in a while). If you compete on service you have a better chance of maintaining a customer base, but with humor they love you and they love to come back! Use humor in your business dealings and not only will current customers love you, but they will tell their friends.

Think of the hot retailers today. They are stores that are fun to shop at. The Disney Store and Warner Brothers are breaking all sorts of records, doing almost $750 per square foot (according to *Time*) while most other shopping mall merchants are happy with $250 per square foot. What is Disney selling? A T-shirt with a rat on it. Does anyone really need anything that these stores are selling? No. Yet you can't walk by one of these stores without the urge to walk in and play. It isn't even gadgets to play with that attract customers, it's just the fun itself!

Rick recently spoke to The Dollar Tree Stores, a chain that sells merchandise for what the name implies: a buck. Does anyone go into a dollar store because they need something? No way. You go in to have fun and poke around. Trust me, no one leaves the store with just one item.

One of the best, most fun merchants in this country today is in the Boston area. Jordan's Furniture is a family business selling mid-range furniture lines. What Jordan's did to differentiate itself in the highly competitive furniture business was to install an amusement park ride, the kind where the seats move with the action on the screen. It is called MOM (Motion Odyssey Movie ride). Elliot and Barry, the funloving owners of the business, keep advertising to come ride MOM. A ticket costs $4.00 and there is usually a wait. Are they making money on the ride? NO. The money goes to a different charity every month. What a great grassroots advertising campaign. Everyone wants to have fun, and the added bonus of making a charitable contribution while having that fun makes it all the better. The store is impressive, but the thing you remember most about Jordan's is the unique, fun attraction in the store.

Elliot and Barry are saying, "Come to our store to have fun. If you buy furniture, that's okay, too." Rick was impressed the night his three teenage kids got three carloads of friends to travel 50 minutes to go to a furniture store. They came back and told Margie and Rick how awesome it was and that they should go. Where do you think these kids are going to buy furniture when they are ready? Rick and Margie were so impressed that they drove the 50 minutes to go on this ride. Rick got the worst headache and upset stomach on MOM, but on the way out of the store they bought two lamps. They went only to have a good time. They didn't really need the lamps, but since they were already there.... And besides, they were in a good mood after the ride.

Someone probably told Barry and Elliot that spending a million dollars-plus on a ride like that was crazy. Crazy like a fox, I think they call it. How would you like people coming to your business because it was fun? How would you like them to be in a good mood and less resistant to the idea of spending money? Not a bad idea, is it?

RECAP:

- We do business with people we have fun with.

- What people in business do you enjoy being around?

- Do people have fun with you or your organization?

- Humor creates business/customer loyalty. What examples can you think of at your company that illustrate this point? How can this be duplicated or expanded upon on a regular basis?

- Humor sells! We repeat this message over and over so get used to it. Start noticing advertisements, attitudes, and appearances that utilize the humor concept.

- Positive humor is an ageless common denominator. Everybody loves to laugh. The marketplace is enormous. Recall the times both you and your children or even the neighbor's kid all laughed together.

- Bottom line: Rick and Margie went to have fun...and ended up with two lamps.

Ideas this gives you for your business:

_____

_____

_____

_____

_____

CHAPTER 19

Grazie, Kevin?

Price deflection—you can have higher prices

---

*"Laughter softens conflicts
in price objections."*

– Rick & Darren

E verybody wants it for less. We are trained to ask for a better price, and why not? It's only natural. Good business people question every price, and they should. However, many people ask out of habit to test the waters. The response signals their next plan of attack. Any time anyone asks our speaking fee they generally follow up with, "Why so much?" or "That's a lot of money," or "I don't think it's in the budget," or "Yeah, but how much for me?"

Too many times people get insulted by requests to lower a price. They have a tendency to take it personally. Laugh it off! How many times have people done this to us and we don't even realize it? Replace the serious or tense emotion with a deflection of humor. Start with a hearty laugh and agree that the fee is high, then proceed with, "Isn't that terrible how prices keep on going up?" Fees like that usually aren't in anybody's budget but somehow they get paid. Silly isn't it? What's money? It's only a thing that we use—it can't even buy us happiness. If I was stranded on a desert island, money is not something I would be yearning for. The "how much for me" question should always be answered with, "10 percent more for you because we are so close. I know you would want me to do so well that I can give more money to charity."

I love it when clients come back with, "Is that your best price?" My reply is a quick, definite, "No. My best price is much higher." At that point they are scratching their heads as you laugh with them. This is the one time you take advantage of the humor perception. If you are laughing it can't be that serious. What's the big deal?

Will you win all negotiations with this strategy? No. But you will avoid a number of confrontations and get your price more times than not. Studies have recently shown us that the majority of people who ask for a lower price ask only once. If we are successful at deflecting the request, the likelihood of being asked a second time for a reduction is slim. Most people don't like to negotiate but do it because they have been told to do it. By using this deflection you get the issue out of the way.

We feel a little guilty using humor in this fashion. We are using the power of humor as a deceptive tool. It is the same as dressing up as a police officer and then robbing a bank. You believe a policeman represents the law so you let him do things you would not allow another person to do. Humor is thought of as light, frivolous, and not to be taken seriously. So when it is used in dealing with a serious subject such as price, it changes the mood to a less defensive atmosphere, which is more conducive to an agreeable behavior.

Think of it from the buyer's side for a moment. You go out to dinner at a fancy Italian restaurant. Your waiter starts speaking broken English. He appears to be imported directly from Italy. He makes up for his communication gap with enthusiasm and entertainment. You find his table tricks and personality to be very funny. So you want to see him do well and you find yourself pulling for the underdog. Your meal is good, not great. After dessert, he hands you the check. It's a bit more than you were expecting, but okay. You look farther down the check to see that it has been signed, "Grazie, Kevin." Kevin? From Italy?

Though the prices at the restaurant were high, when you got into the car and drove home what did you talk about? The prices? Most people at this particular restaurant leave talking about Kevin and how much fun he was. Next time they come back (with friends), they ask for Kevin. He has his own band of regulars. How much is he really worth to that restaurant?

Kevin is actually a friend of Rick and Darren's. He is also a professional clown with oodles of talent and was the star of an improvisational show. Kevin is not Italian. Not even close, but he pulls it off like no one else can. Kevin successfully deflects the price by making dinner more about the experience. His entertainment absorbs some of the price barriers. We've seen people wait longer to be served by Kevin. As for this *Laugh & Get Rich* lesson, Grazie, Kevin!

RECAP:

- Everyone wants it for less.
- Laugh off the request in a complimentary manner.
- Include your opposing negotiator in the laughter.
- Humor breaks down the barrier and derails the other's train of thought.
- Humor is sometimes enough to satisfy the price request without harder negotiations.

- What type of negotiations do you do in which humor could be your ally?
- Which of your opposing negotiator's trains of thought do you want to derail?
- Think of it from the buyer's side.
- How could you deflect the price of your product or service?
- What might Kevin do if he worked for you?

Ideas this gives you for your business:

CHAPTER 20

"Please, Please, Call Me Back... It's Important!"

Be the first to be called back

"All messages are not created equal."

– Rick Segel

How often do you try to reach someone only to leave countless messages? Not returning calls is unprofessional, but many times people who are in buying situations are inundated with sales calls of all kinds. Even if they are not buyers, time has become the currency of the day. Some people just don't have enough time to return all the calls they receive and must prioritize whom they will be calling back. So in reality, you are selling yourself to get a call back. If speaking to someone directly is necessary to doing business, then you have to get their attention. And you have to do it without being or becoming the world's largest pain in the...whatever you want to call it. What's the solution? Do it with humor!

What's the first goal? To speak to them. How can you get them on the phone and smiling when they call you back? The second goal? You want them receptive, as well. Think of the individuals you are trying to reach. What do their desks look like when they return from two minutes away from it? They usually have a stack of the standard pink message pad call-backs, with three marked IMPORTANT sitting beside a half-full cold cup of coffee, which, in turn, sits next to a phone filled with voice mail messages. Why would they want to return your call first? How do you make it different, uncommon, unique, interesting, exciting, funny, or—most important—effective?

Don't do what everyone else does. Don't just leave your name and number. Make it memorable. How, you ask? Use Rick's line when a gatekeeper asks who he is. "Oh, I'm Mr. Smith's 97th most favorite client," he says. The usual response to this is a request to further identify yourself. Rick will say, "Well don't you know who the 96th is? I'm the one right after." Of course you eventually let them know who you are, but don't be afraid to use the grabbing line, "I am your 97th most favorite client and DEMAND to be treated that way." The gatekeeper will have a good laugh and never forget you.

Keep people off guard. Do the unusual. Darren and Rick recently sat in the audience to hear D.J. Harrington, an international expert in the area of telephone power. D.J. does something unique whenever he can't get a phone call returned. He faxes a giant "while you were out" sheet. It looks the same as the small pink padded message, however the size is 8-1/2 by 11 inches. This has impact. Now picture that same desk. Which message note has the most impact with the most humor? Obviously, the big one, but the impact is not from the size alone. It's the creativity used in the process. Everyone is going to say "Hey look at this fax!" More people will look at the fax, talk about it, and even ask the recipient "Did you call that person back with the big message?" People want to call back because it's fun. Getting that fax might be the highlight of the day. In some offices it might be the highlight of the year. Before that person calls you back, they are already in a good mood. They are expecting you to be creative, interesting, and fun.

If that isn't enough, D.J. takes it a step further with the old line, "I spoke to God this morning, why can't I speak to you?" It works for him. Rick doesn't use it because he doesn't talk to God that much. We prefer lines like, "Please call, I have to go to the bathroom soon." Or come up with a good line yourself and call us. We are collecting good messages to write in the blank of the message pad. Send us one and maybe it will end up in our next book.

This is but one type of humorous fax sheet, of which there have been so many. Books have been written on just that! Humor works. People will read fun faxes 68 percent more often than serious faxes. (Actually, we just made up those statistics, but they sound good, don't they? It beats doing the research, and as long as we make light of the truth, no one gets mad and we keep our credibility—if we have any!) Research has also proven that the majority of all fun faxes are either saved by the recipient, passed on, or faxed over to someone else.

So why don't more people use fun faxes? We don't know. Maybe the person is boring or likes being in the back of the herd of cattle. Different sells! When was the last time you heard anyone in a retail store saying, "That's the same old thing, let's buy it"? They don't! They say, "I haven't seen that before," and then they buy it.

Is voice mail a curse or a blessing? We believe it's a wonderful humortunity (get it? humor + opportunity = humortunity). Let us explain and share a story that attests to the power of humor when applied to the technology of voice mail. Rick believes that voice mail is the greatest invention of mankind, next only to the microwave oven. He believes that a voice message is more than a message, it is a 30-second commercial to sell your product. Humor sells, we've established that. Why not use humor to work for you here? All it takes is a little creativity.

Rick has been preaching this concept in all his seminars for a long time and telling it to his wife, partner, marketing person, and all-around office manager (all that would be Margie). At first she was very reluctant to use this concept. Rick kept on reminding her, but still she would not try. Until one day out of sheer disgust she said, "You do it!" She explained that she had one contact she had been trying to get on the phone for the longest time who just wouldn't call back.

This was perfect for Rick. He made the call. The outgoing message said, "You have reached the Bat Line. If you wish to leave a message, do so after the beep." Rick thought, "This guy is fun for using the Bat Line in his message. I'll have some fun!" Rick's message was, "Batman, before you slide down the Bat Pole and drive off in the Batmobile, call Robin and Cat Woman (a.k.a. Rick or Margie Segel), who will be waiting in the Bat Cave." He then gave his phone number. Within an hour the man called back laughing. He said, "That was great! No one ever did that to us before!"

Rick thought he had to be kidding. Could he have really been the only one? No way! Then Rick realized that the organization he had called was the Big And Tall association. They both had a good laugh, and a year later Rick spoke at that association.

Does humor messaging work? You bet, and a relationship was created because of that one 22-second message. It had made all the difference.

RECAP:

- Goal: get someone to call you back.
- Tool: use humor to get people to call you back.
- Do something different...do something fun.
- Humor sets a tone for a more effective call.
- Everyone leaves messages. How many leave a message with a fax?
- What ideas can you think of that will help you humorize your message?
- The big message fax works great, but with a clever line it's even better.
- Voice mail = humortunity.

Ideas this gives you for your business:

CHAPTER 21

The Auntie Factor

Inclusionary humor

"If you choose one characteristic to carry through your career, choose a sense of humor."
– Darren & Rick

Rick asked his wife how to spell inclusionary and she said it wasn't a word! He didn't believe her. He checked dictionary after dictionary and even the computer's spell check. Nothing! A great "Ah-ha!" came from Rick. The creation of another new word and phrase. We define it as humor that includes people who might not normally or necessarily be included. It includes people in the creation of the humor or the humorous event.

One example of great inclusionary humor is the interactive wedding show craze. The play itself is only 20 minutes long, but the rest of the show is completely interactive. A cast of 15 characters is constantly working the tables trying to get as many people involved as possible. The cast is the actual wedding party. This isn't new theater—it has been done since Shakespeare's day, but with a different twist. The difference is that the audience is also playing a part. They are the relatives and friends of the bride and groom. People are not used to being part of the humor, so when they are, the laugh is that much greater.

One comment Darren received in playing the groom's role was, "I loved the groom the best because he called me Auntie." Darren made her part of the show and she will never forget her experience because of that. Inclusionary humor has a magnifying effect on the experience because you are part of the show or a part of what is going on.

Don't we all hate it when we walk into a room at a party and everyone is talking about something and no one takes the time to explain to you what they are talking about? You feel left out. When someone gives you that brief update of what everyone is talking about you feel as if you can contribute and start to get involved. That feeling we just described is bad enough, but when humor is involved and you're not part of the process you almost feel as if the joke is on or about you. You feel like a piece of moldy pie.

It doesn't take a rocket scientist to figure out that if you feel bad by not being included, you will feel good if you are included. Trust us! Darren and Rick know the feeling of always being the last kids picked in the schoolyard. Self-esteem goes right down the tubes. When Darren was in grammar school, his mother dressed him in a red corduroy cape, similar to the kind Sherlock Holmes wore, with a matching cap. His mother thought it was adorable. The other kids taunted him: "Darren, Darren, the Red Baron." Rick once got traded for the right to have the water jug at the team's bench. Can you imagine getting traded for that! Persecution is a great trainer of humor.

What we have outlined is basically the premise of Dr. Norman Cousins' philosophy in his book *Anatomy of an Illness*. If bad things make you feel bad, then good things make you feel good. Everyone who speaks on humor uses the work of Dr. Norman Cousins, and you may want to add his book to your library.

If you can bring people closer to you by including them in your humor, why wouldn't you do it? Why wouldn't you include your customers in what you are laughing at? Wouldn't they take ownership in the humor? You might just be surprised at how well they can relate to the subject and even contribute one of their own stories. This will radically increase the likelihood of them becoming closer, more loyal, and better customers.

Rick has produced a training video for the retail industry called *Stop Losing Retail Sales*. It includes a segment about inclusionary humor on the retail sales floor. The video shows two sales clerks laughing about a TV sitcom when a customer walks in the store. They stop laughing and go into their selling mode. Because they stopped their conversation abruptly, the customer feels a little left out. There is another segment with the two sales clerks sharing the same story with the customer. The customer laughs, adds something to the story, and any sales resistance is gone. It was an instant bonding with the customer. What could be better?

One of the subjects that Rick speaks about is how to profile your customers—in short, how you can learn as much information as possible about the person you are dealing with and use it to further your sales relationship. By having your customer share a story you begin to know more about your own clientele and how they think. Rick believes that you should not only find out a person's birthday, anniversary, number of children, hobbies, and so on, but also find out what makes the person laugh. Who is their favorite comedian or funny person and what do they do for fun? Does this give you any ideas about an effective "thank you" holiday gift?

RECAP:

- Involving people makes a greater impact.

- Inclusionary humor is a new word and phrase. Understand it and use it to your advantage.

- If not being included makes you feel bad, then being included should make you feel good.

- Find out what type of humor your customer likes so you can include them in what they like.

- Involve clients or customers as part of the show or experience. Don't just include them, involve them.

- What might be your next humor holiday gift to clients?

Ideas this gives you for your business:

_____

_____

_____

_____

_____

_____

_____

_____

_____

CHAPTER 22

The Rule of the Unexpected

Surprise!

"Sylvia, the head of lettuce is talking!"

– Meeting attendee

Predictability is boring! We struggled over that first sentence for about 15 minutes (well, it really wasn't that long, but you know Darren, he likes to over-dramatize). Marriages go sour because they become monotonous. People leave jobs because of boredom. People fall asleep in meetings because of predictability and lack of anything exciting to keep them focused. People fall asleep reading a book if there is nothing exciting to keep their interest.

That is why we keep on throwing in asides: to make you, our reader, feel part of what we are doing, and jabbing you with small humor points that stimulate the mind. This is not meant to be a joke book. We are just trying to make the content interesting and light. That was the reason we wrote the aside about Darren to open this chapter. It was different and brought you closer to us—to Darren especially. If we succeeded we hoped it would create that tiny smile or grin on your face. All humor isn't the belly laugh. Humor is the natural attention-getter and keeper, as we discuss many times. If you pick up any how-to romance book, it always says that if you do the unexpected, you will become more romantic.

What we propose is that if you do the unexpected, you will become the life of the situation, a burst of revitalization. Just like that kid in high school who dropped his tray and lost it all in front of everyone. You felt bad, but you giggled and talked about it for the rest of lunch. Just like that shock jock who says something outrageous on your commute to work that gets people going.

It mystifies us why most corporate brainstorming sessions are held in very non-creative work environments, like the corporate boardroom. We have decided that the reason they are called boardrooms is because most people who attend meetings there are bored, which is easy to see given their familiar surroundings. People go into these brainstorming sessions to get the organization out of the corner they painted themselves into. The irony is, to get out of the corner we hold meetings in a rectangular room with a rectangular table and four rectangular walls. There is a rectangular flip chart next to the rectangular white board being illuminated by rectangular florescent lights, and everyone is taking notes on rectangular paper, which we take out of our rectangular briefcase. Then they ask us to think out of the box. Would that be a rectangular box?

Okay, so you're not going to spend $50,000 to change the box. We have some ways of adding creativity to the most boring of boxes. At a function run by your authors (Rick and Darren) held in your typical Marriott hotel sliding-wall function room (rectangular), we wanted to set the mood for an evening. The function was the Saturday night stress reliever in the middle of a weekend conference. The mood had to be set from the outset. The key was the unexpected.

The structure of the evening was to start off with an hors d'oeuvres table and cocktails. So far, nothing out of the ordinary, but our purpose was to make the ordinary unordinary. On the line for hors d'oeuvres we had strategically placed four heads of lettuce. The difference was that these heads were human heads decorated with lettuce, their faces painted green. As an unsuspecting guest passed by, the head said things such as, "Feed me," or "You're taking too much food," or "Watch your cholesterol."

The shock quickly turned to laughter and the next thing you saw were the guests' leaving their plate of food to get their friends and show them what they had discovered so they could see their friends' reactions. The mood was set. To make it interactive, signs were placed near our talking heads of lettuce that read, "Please do not feed the heads of lettuce," which led to interesting antics as "the heads" asked people to disobey the signs (that's Inclusionary humor, too). There was a study in human nature!

The warm-up act had done its job in the most unexpected place. The crowd got involved, the event was memorable, and tension was relieved, even before the night had officially begun. The talking heads served as the warm-up act for the humorists who followed. Very little had to be done to get this crowd in the mood for relaxation and laughter.

RECAP:

- Break your normal routine with the unexpected. What routines are you and the people around you too familiar with? How can you create the unexpected? Easiest question to start with, "What will they expect?"

- Set the tone of "difference" right off the bat.

- Where could the lettuce head idea work for you?

- How do you start brainstorming sessions? How could you start them next time?

- If the bottom line is the bottom line is it worth the effort?

Ideas this gives you for your business:

_____

_____

_____

_____

_____

_____

_____

_____

_____

_____

CHAPTER 23

Yes, But My Product Is DIFFERENT!!!

All the more reason to use humor

"Busy People are HAPPY people!"

– Thelma Green, RN (Rick's mother-in-law)

Some of you may be reading this and saying, "Humor may work for many products or services, but not mine!" We have not yet come across one instance in which we can't find a way that humor could help in some aspect of the business. The reason is, business is about people and relationships. When you think of filling your gas tank, do you think fun?

People are lazy and impatient by nature. In these fast-paced days, products and services are becoming more human-nature–focused to stay competitive. A few years ago no one would have guessed that paying at the pump would be a major advantage for a gas station. Convenience is king! Time is becoming more and more valuable to an ever-increasing segment of our population.

The vast majority of us prefers to pay at the pump. So what does that have to do with a book about the use of humor in business? More than you think. Every station that got the equipment to pay at the pump saw an immediate increase in sales. That is, until all the other stations got the same equipment. Then it was no longer a WOW item, it was a necessity.

Those of us who wish to pump our own gas usually go through the same routine time and again. We select a grade, insert the nozzle, then let our mind and our eyes wander as the gas is pumping, agonizing over the wait (especially in the bitter cold winter). This process had seemed an unavoidable fact of life. Then Darren visited a Shell gas station in town and saw Lucy. *I Love Lucy*, that is. The dealer actually has a video monitor in front of you to watch while you pump. Darren found himself mesmerized as he went through this previously mundane task. The show starts when you pick up the handle and shuts down when you replace it. Is that customer service or what?

What a difference that made to Darren and the other people at neighboring pumps. Maybe that's why Shell named their stores ETD (Experience The Difference). Everyone had this big grin on their faces and it stayed there while they got back in their cars. The company didn't have to use *I Love Lucy*, and it no longer does. Instead, it spent hundreds of thousands of dollars to create its own fun spots. These spots are produced just to be played at a gas pump. What Shell figured out, after spending thousands of dollars in customer surveys, is that its customers don't know the difference between its product and its competition's. Therefore, Shell must differentiate itself another way.

Shell knew that its customers wanted quick and easy dealings when they came in for gas. The challenge to Shell was defining "quick" from the customer's point of view. The answer? It was the perception of time, not the actual time spent, that mattered. First, Shell took a normally boring task and made it enjoyable. Second, it came up with an idea that definitely differentiates it from the gas station across the street and increases loyalty.

Do you think this would impact sales? The most important impact I noticed was the effect on the average order size. While Darren was in this trance, he became less aware of the money he was spending on this particular fill-up. Also, the experience can produce a cliffhanger type effect. As you watch, you might want to see what happens next on the show. Darren doesn't even remember what the gas price was. The people he saw left the gas station with a smile on their faces. Do you think this was just a friendly gesture or do you think there is an intrinsic impact on the bottom line? Is that a feeling you would like your customers to leave with?

Footnote to this chapter: Darren wrote this almost a full year before Rick got a training contract to work with all the Shell cashiers in New England. Little did we know how perceptive Darren was when he simply made a comment through the eyes of a customer. He never realized he was part of a statistical majority that Shell paid the prestigious Wharton School of Finance to study. Kudos to Darren for reaching almost the identical conclusions after only a few minutes at the pump. Shell is actually changing its corporate direction based on some of these findings. The company might not call it the use of humor, but whatever they call it, these videos distract the mind of the consumer and makes the time fly by. So if you are thinking that humor cannot help your product or service, think again!

RECAP:

- If you can add humor to pumping gas, you and your company have no excuses!

- Every second of your customer's time is valuable. Respect it!

- Where is your customer's attention when waiting?

- How could you amuse your customers to make waiting time pass more effortlessly?

- More important, how could you use their time to add to your bottom line?

Ideas this gives you for your business:

CHAPTER 24

Bathroom Humor... Redefined

The captive audience

"Some of the best ideas come from the strangest places—so, make more strange places!"

– Rick Segel

This chapter is NOT just for men! And it's not about dirty jokes. It's about the universal, laughter-generating common denominator. For all of you who think we are going too far, we aren't. We didn't create this phenomenon, we are merely observers of what makes people laugh. However, there is another interesting thing that takes place while driving, on the john, or in the shower. People usually come up with their best ideas under these circumstances.

Anytime Rick does a presentation about humor in the workplace, he asks the audience where they come up with their best ideas. There is a pause, then one or two people start to laugh. You know what they are going to say. When they say "the toilet," everyone starts to laugh because they have the same experience. Is it because we are in a relaxed state? Is it because we are relieving tension? Does the john represent something funny? Why is it so contradictory that a room with such utilitarian qualities allows creative thinking? Is it the meditation that we just don't get to do?

We believe that as good as the john is for creative ideas, it falls short in the ability for brainstorming sessions. We believe that every office should have a john in the middle of the work area. Just sit down and think. After all, what do you think Rodin's subject is doing in the famous sculpture *The Thinker*? He is on the hopper. If the sculpture were really lifelike you would see a roll of toilet paper beside him.

Enough of this frivolous stuff. Maybe this chapter is the comic relief of the book, but perhaps what we should be doing is analyzing this laughter so we can harness the tension-relieving and creative qualities that the bathroom just naturally brings out of us. Let's make it work. How?

Some men's rooms, usually in pubs or even in nice hotels, put the sports pages on a bulletin board over the urinals or on the back of stall doors. (This idea might be used at the office as the best place to put office memos, because here at least the chances increase that they will get read.) This practice is okay if the home team wins, but if the team loses it has a negative effect on one's attitude or mood.

We have already established the fact that humor relaxes and puts people in a good mood. It also bonds people together. Think about what would happen if you had a joke, gag, cartoon, or funny one-liner page in every bathroom in the office or any gathering place. People would then have something in common. Sometimes, for teamwork to occur, all you need is that common ground or topic for two people to share. It starts with, "Did you see that...?" and progresses from there.

What if, two or three times a week, a list was posted on the inside door of the john and above the urinals? What you'd have is a mini-humor break. This is what we mean by humorizing the bathroom. People leave happy and more creative. Maybe they will have forgotten that they were upset about something before they went to the bathroom. We are cleaning the slate by deflecting the mind during a relaxed state. It makes sense: people clean out their bladders, why not clean out the mind?

Another idea we just thought about while in the john. How about having a small note pad and pencil in the john for those great ideas you might forget? You can capture that moment of inspiration. It's almost as good as a Kodak moment, but it adds profits. We call it, "The Moment of Inspirational Dumping." Let's not lose sight of the obvious: the bathroom is the one place everyone goes. It's the perfect setting for some gentle distraction.

RECAP:

- Bathroom humor is universal.

- Bathroom humor can and should be *clean.*

- The best ideas occur while driving and in the bathroom. How can you capture these ideas?

- Take advantage of natural humor and manipulate to your purposes: PRODUCTIVITY.

- The one place visited every day by everyone (the ones who are regular).

- Puts people in the right frame of mind.

- The laugh of the day on all the back doors of all the stalls of all the johns.

Ideas this gives you for your business:

_____

_____

_____

_____

_____

_____

_____

_____

CHAPTER 25

Wait Management
Lose wait fast! And no diet pills!

"We hate to wait!"

– Everyone

D oesn't it just fry you when you phone the service department of a company and they answer, "Service, please hold." Then they keep you on hold for 5 minutes. One of the most highly emotional pet peeves is the waiting game. No one likes to wait. It upsets our clients, potential clients, and shows a lack of consideration for the value of their time. In the words of Dan Burrus, the famous futurist, "The currency of the '90s and beyond is time."

Therefore, good customer service focuses on shortening the length of time required for people to wait. Great customer service is *no* waiting, or at least the giving the perception of no waiting. We all try for that, however that's not always possible. If you know your business becomes extra busy during only one hour a day, such as lunchtime if you operate a restaurant, it might not be financially feasible to hire extra people to work just the one hour each day. This puts you in the military mode of customer service, gauging your success on a scale of acceptable losses. Sorry, no loss is acceptable.

Humor to the rescue! Can't you hear the sound of the bugle, the galloping hooves from the single, sleek white horse (and a bunch of brown ones), the shouts of the cavalry, and the jokester helping customers wait without minding it. Stop. Humor can do all of that and so much more. It can make people actually like waiting. They don't want to stop waiting. They just want to keep on listening to the distraction that entertainment—specifically, humor—can bring. Yes, entertainment does make the time seem shorter than it is, but more important, it replaces bad time with good time and sends the message that you care. Humor is a great stress reliever and therefore aids in the smooth flow of business. This reinforces one of our earlier premises: that humor is the great social lubricator.

The use of humor in a waiting situation can help to avoid the stress issue altogether. Certainly the situation creates a strong prognosis for the occurrence of stress, but it can be completely avoided with the proper dosage of humor, before stress can rear its ugly head and sever a client relationship. Though we cannot control what happens in the lives of the people we make wait, we can control the environment in which they wait.

Take a good, long look at your waiting "game room" (or reception area). What do you see? I know, I know, you have to remain professional...but this is about the bottom line! Maybe you have games or coloring books for the little kids? What about the big kids? The ones with stress on their faces who have come to see you and been told to "just have a seat, it will only be a minute." What do you have for them? The latest newsmagazines? That should help! Reading about destruction and corruption is just what they need to relieve tension—plus you just asked them to wait and they are already running behind. Oh, that will set a nice tone before all of your meetings! Are we suggesting that you get rid of those tension-building magazines? Absolutely! Most waiting rooms have those. Don't you want to be different? Changes must be made to improve the culture of your organization. Rick says to throw that stuff out and burn it. Why? Because at least the heat from the fire would be comforting, and the beauty of the flame, soothing.

Break it down: Where do people wait? In offices, on the phone, at a bus stop, in a line, at a transportation terminal, and in the ubiquitous waiting room. Why do they even call it that? It does nothing to aid in waiting other than providing some outdated magazines. A delivery room helps you deliver a baby; a meeting room helps you meet by having aids such as blackboards, easels, slide projectors, and screens. The waiting room does nothing. Most people and most companies put no effort into waiting room management. The time has come to change all of this. Darren and Rick to the rescue!

How can a company say it cares about people and do little or nothing to ease the heartache of the waiting room blues? Why would you want a person who comes to see you become down or depressed after reading about a terrorist attack, a plane crash, or a kidnapping? Then we offer them coffee. Ooh, caffeine. Let's add that to the mix!

Keep people happy, and even if they are there to sell you something, at least they will be more pleasant to deal with. You can influence their attitudes before they even see you, and that can lead to hidden profits. When someone is in a good mood, their defenses are down and they just might offer you a price they might not have offered if they were more tense. Don't we do more for people we like? We do, and we believe most other people do as well.

Let people know you care about them in a waiting room by providing the distractions that some companies are starting to do. An orthodontist in Boston put video games in his waiting room. (Of course, now the kids never want to leave the waiting room.) What about putting in headsets of different comedians in concert? We should all take a lesson from Disney. They work at line management. They have characters entertaining you in lines as you wait in Florida's 95-degree temperatures. They have TV monitors strategically placed above you so your wait becomes as enjoyable as the event.

Two weeks ago, Rick went to MGM Studios in Orlando. It was a slow time with very few people in the park. He whipped right through the *Star Wars* ride without waiting. Having been on the ride before, it wasn't as much fun without the wait. You miss all the diversions set up to help you heighten the enjoyment of the experience. Simply put, it wasn't as much fun going on more rides in less time without the waits, which have become a part of the riding experience.

How is your waiting room decorated? Does it give off an upbeat feeling? What colors do you use? Do you have any interactive games to play? What about some fun quotes on the wall? Most important, is the person who greets visitors to your waiting room an official company greeter or whoever happens to be there at the time? Is your greeter passive or proactive about controlling the attitude of the people waiting?

Darren went to interview Jim Laffey, CEO of Color for Real Estate (a printing company), who is the epitome of the *Laugh & Get Rich* philosophy. "Wait Management" is an area in which this company shines (but they are so great in all areas that all of Chapter 43 is dedicated to them). Before Darren met Jim, he walked through the company's waiting area. Darren knew he was in the right place. As he looked around, the smile of approval on his face grew. Not many waiting rooms have rubber chickens hanging in them; a beautiful reminder to employees and customers of the importance of humor in your day.

This, however, was just the beginning. One of the walls is covered with fun prizes. Every customer walks out with one. Expensive? How much is a customer worth? Darren looked down and discovered he was standing on artificial turf. Different, yes, but functional, too. He was standing on a putting green! They had a putting machine. Putt while you wait! How cool. But that's not all! Color for Real Estate employees are encouraged to bring their dogs to work. They really do treat everyone like family there. If they are straight out busy and the customer's order is not ready, one of the customer service representatives asks the waiting customer to take the dog for a walk and hands over the leash. The dumbfounded customer doesn't quite know what to do and figures if it will help them keep working on the order.... The magic is that they have never had a customer come back without a smile after taking a dog for a walk.

This is an example to stretch your thinking about what is possible, professional, and effective. Even if you don't have an actual waiting room, think about your theoretical or virtual waiting room. What about your back orders? What can you do? Employees who deal directly with these clients are a gold mine of untapped ideas. Do you think it is a coincidence that golf was part of Color for Real Estate's plan? Golf is prevalent in the professional world. Animal lovers are equally numerous.

What are some of the common hobbies or interests that your customers share, or that you share with your customers. Some cynics might say, "What about non-golfers and people who are allergic to animals?" To them, Rick and Darren say, "You're right! Don't ever change a thing. Stay in your comfort zone. Give this book to your competition and go back to the chapter on Funsuckers." Not all customers love these extras, but those who do are more apt to spread the word about you and bring their friends into your company's bottom line.

How else do you keep your internal and external customers waiting? Those are the trouble spots. Focus on more than just the waiting room. Many companies do not actually have reception areas, but clients still experience the "wait hate." These times are actually relationship enhancing opportunities. What do people complain about when they get to customer service? How can you strategically defuse those complaints ahead of time? When people have to wait for you or your company, chances are they experience the same thing with your competition. Who handles waiting better? This is a great chance to differentiate your company from others.

Although many companies bring in speakers on stress management, few take an active role in managing the stress of their clients. People remember best what they are most emotional about. Let it be positive rather than negative. Let the negative be with the competition, not with you. Take an active role in starving the life out of stress and keep it from growing.

When Darren first called Color for Real Estate, a delightful, energetic young woman, Karen, answered the phone, spoke to him for a minute, and then asked if she could put him on hold. To Darren's surprise, the hold music was the theme to *The Beverly Hillbillies.* That's right! "Wanna tell you a story 'bout a man named Jed...." A smile came across Darren's face, which quickly turned into a silly grin. With his nose for customer service and belief in Wait Management, Darren nearly jumped out of his skin with enthusiasm. These people get it, he thought, better than Rick and I ever dreamed! Humor is one thing, but humor and music hit much deeper! Color for Real Estate's music-on-hold includes theme songs from popular TV shows of the past, such as *The Addams Family, Flipper,* and *The Jetsons* (the CEO's favorite). Think about the genius in this. These songs evoke warm, fun memories of childhood—the Clown Concept, hard at work, melting stress away.

When Karen came back on the line, Darren's first words were, "How can anyone get frustrated with you after listening to that song!" She replied, "No one usually does." Wow, talk about a tool for business! This company has one-upped our idea about putting comedy routines in place of chamber music on hold.

Darren immediately started interviewing Karen about the reactions they get from clients. He was told that at least three times a day people ask to be put back on hold. BACK ON HOLD?!? It was no joke. Karen said that more often she is asked what song the customer heard. She and her co-workers have to explain that they can't hear the music, so they don't know. Ever had a song in your head you can't identify? Well, these customers frequently hum (or sing) the song to help facilitate in identifying it. This leads to all sorts of fun and play, which helps form a bond between the customer and the company. Darren was told that this has helped their customer service department immeasurably. The company has even had entire offices call on speakerphone to ask to be put on hold.

This example has helped us to focus on the earlier idea of humor on hold. What is the age range of your target market? Who are the favorite childhood comedians of that generation? How about putting them on hold? People hate to wait. Wherever there is tension in your business, there is an opportunity to make your business more successful than it already is. Identify these areas and focus on alleviating that stress. Would you want to do business with you?

RECAP:

- The perception of waiting is worse than the wait.
- Where in your business do you make people wait? Are you making it an enjoyable wait?
- What other distracters can you use to make a wait more enjoyable?
- You have a captive audience; find a creative way to educate them about your business.
- Practice Wait Management. How can you use humor as a remedy?
- Make this a place to WOW your customer and drive your competition crazy!
- Avoid the waiting room blues. Eliminate what kind of material?
- What effect would showing humor tapes have? Or a promo video about the company?
- Take a proactive role. Starve stress or it will grow like a bad weed.
- Where might your customers experience wait hate?

Ideas this gives you for your business:

_____

_____

_____

_____

_____

CHAPTER 26

Al vs. the Comedian

Know thy customer, custom humor is king

"Humor Is in the Mind of the Beholder."

– Darren La Croix

K nowing the people you are communicating with, whether via memo, advertising, or a presentation, is important to the success of your message. Commonalities such as how they think, how they feel about issues facing them, and their pet peeves can be bay windows of opportunity (which are much bigger than the normal windows of opportunity). If you can hit home, your message is more likely to be heard. If you do not hit home, you are probably wasting your time and effort.

A very funny friend of Darren's, Al Ziehl, is a sales manager for a major electronics company. Recently, Al was in charge of setting up a large and entertaining program for his salespeople and staff. Al hired a comedian who had appeared on *The Tonight Show* more than once (at the top of his profession—no slouch). Before the event, Al met with the comedian to give him the inside scoop on the audience and where they were coming from. The comedian declined the offer of this information. The show went very well and the audience enjoyed themselves. What happened next was the ironic part. After the comedian had left the stage, Al himself proceeded to entertain the troops. He leveled them with laughter. He floored the place. It was as if he had a magical power that the comedian did not possess.

That magical power is real: he knew the audience better. He knew these people because he worked with these people. He knew their common frustrations. He had a good feel for the sales staff's perceptions of the company and its upper management. Although the comedian was very good and his timing well-honed, he had addressed the commonalities these people had as humans, not the closer ties they shared as business associates. And although Al is funny, he had never performed stand-up comedy. But the tool Al used was more powerful and has more potential than years of practice can offer.

What are the common frustrations and pet peeves that people have in your company? What about your customers? Before we present to any company it is imperative that we get background information so that we speak to our audiences in their terms and with their values in mind. That's when humor works the best—when you know your audience better then they know themselves.

THE BEST MATERIAL IS WRITTEN
15 MINUTES BEFORE A SPEECH

Why? Because of the common bond that creates universal laughter in any organization. You are in the moment, flush with what everyone together has just experienced. This is the hot stuff, the fresh donuts. You are in real time. No one will ever accuse you of giving a canned speech, because the audience believes you are impromptu.

The best example is a speech that Rick gave in Ontario. Whereas Rick is nearly bald, the woman who spoke before him was a very attractive young woman with long, straight hair, which she wore tucked behind her ears. While she was delivering her message her hair kept popping out from behind her ear, so she tucked it back again. She performed that little annoying procedure probably 20 or 25 times.

The first words out of Rick's mouth when he arrived on stage were: "You won't have any hair problems with me!" It brought the house down. Was it a particularly funny line? No. At least not to anyone who wasn't there. To someone arriving late it meant nothing. Darren has built a career out of this principle: he attends association conferences, goes to the sessions, interviews attendees, and on the last night of the convention performs a keynote of customized humor.

We live in a world of mass customization. Customers want it when they want it, how they want it, and where they want it. Humor and comedy are no exception. The closer to the bone, the more likely you are to split the ribs.

RECAP:

- Being a comedian or being "born funny" is not a prerequisite for making people laugh.

- Knowing your audience's emotional cues are opportunities for effective humor! (These cues can be internal or external.)

- Do you research so you know the people to whom you communicate?

- Learn how to turn commonalities of a group into humor.

- It's what's important to your audience that is important.

- There are different levels of humor; customized is the highest.

Ideas this gives you for your business:

_____

_____

_____

_____

_____

_____

_____

_____

_____

CHAPTER 27

The Humor Detour

The power of the impostor

---

*"Humor is emotional chaos
remembered in tranquility."*

– James Thurber

More and more companies are using impostors at their meetings to shake things up. They want to do something different or to bring the group together. There is no better way of bringing a group together than having them bond over a common humorous incident. The impostor serves that role. The next example demonstrates the strength of impostoring, which can turn a normal meeting into a morale-boosting, team-building experience while providing a good laugh.

The M.O. of the impostor is to first work the crowd and find some real believers and then, when he or she gets up to speak, to aggravate the audience so they unite against the impostor. The impostor is a "put on." He or she is a fictitious keynote industry speaker hired to put one over on the audience and to humor the audience.

Recently, Rick had the honor of speaking to the American Association of Retired Persons (AARP) employment division SCSEP national conference (don't ask what this stands for 'cause I don't think anyone really knows). Rick was the last speaker for a 5-day conference. Its planners wanted to do something different and upbeat. Instead of the traditional motivational or educational type of presentation, this group wanted people to leave the conference with an upbeat, tension-relieving gift of humor and fun. They had just been through a very difficult 5 days. They were facing major government cutbacks just passed through Congress. They were afraid of losing not only some of their programs but also their jobs.

They wanted everyone there to know how important the use of humor was, especially in the current time of crisis. Rick was brought in to deliver this message in a unique way. He was listed on the program as Hamilton Minnifield, Ph.D., from Government Organizations Training Consultants for Hiring and Administration, Inc., located in Cambridge, Massachusetts. (Did you notice the company's acronym? GOTCHA!) Rick was supposed to be an esteemed authority who did extensive work for the Department of Labor. Basically, he was playing a bureaucratic, pompous ass. He was not allowed to smile in front of any participants before his secret was revealed. This was extremely difficult and out of character for Rick.

The people who hired him provided prepared material— inside stuff that only this particular audience would have understood or appreciated. He started off by reading this material and actually got the audience to the point of hostility. He read pages (and pages) from the manual of the Office of Management and Budgets, which if you haven't had the opportunity to read is probably the most boring information ever written by man or woman. He actually yelled at the audience for not memorizing the information! Slowly he let them in on his little charade by looking at their problems from a humorous point of view.

An interesting phenomenon took place. The more tension he gave the audience, the more welcome the tension relief of humor. What happened in that hall was exactly what Dr. Andersen, President of The Devry Institute of Technology, will discuss later in the book. There was a real bonding of people, all coming together and sharing a good belly laugh. Rick doesn't talk about teamwork, but that's what happened. People looked at each other and couldn't stop laughing. What a way to end a conference. It gave people the feeling that they were not alone in their frustrations and anxiety. Not one person left that room without realizing the importance of humor. It was the right medicine for that conference. They left having been rejuvenated by a humorous event they will never forget. One that also brought everyone just a bit closer together.

What took place before the program was also interesting. Some people being introduced to "Dr. Minnifield" were actually trying to network with him or kiss up to him. Rick found it challenging to avoid engaging in any conversation that might damage his cover. Rick double-talked more before the speech than he did during it. The people who spoke to Rick before his presentation experienced the biggest laughs during the show. They felt even more a part of the show. This is the same reaction Darren and Rick have observed when doing the wedding shows.

Our hats are off to the people at AARP for tapping the power of humor to make their conference memorable, creating group cohesion, all the while teaching a valuable lesson—the lesson of humor and its ability to turn a situation around.

RECAP:

- Off beat and different create emotional humor that is memorable.

- The impostor is best when additional stress is created. It makes the release more fun.

- The impostor brings more people into the act with interactions before the presentation.

- The organization that uses this type of tool is generally respected for its creativity.

- Conference attendees are usually on information-overload and need the release.

- Have your people involved in the writing or at least the interview process. It makes them part of the show, too.

- Inclusionary Humor is the goal.

Ideas this gives you for your business:

_____

_____

_____

_____

_____

_____

_____

CHAPTER 28

Oh Boy, Another Staff Meeting

If they snooze, you lose!

"Staff meeting, here we go again."

– Staff member

Most business people have their share of meetings every day. Staff meetings are often attended by less-than-enthusiastic employees. This is where the difficulty occurs. Under such circumstances it is difficult to communicate important information in ways that can easily be retained by your audience.

The human mind tends to retain emotional thoughts best, be these emotions positive or negative. However, very few people are passionately bored (though some see sleeping in a staff meeting as an attempt at this). The tendency of management is to think that just because there is a meeting, employees are ready to receive transmissions from mission control. Because employees at a staff meeting are not being judged on their job performance, minds can begin to drift. But at that meeting you are competing with their thoughts about work they'd rather be doing, or, more likely, about difficulties in their personal lives. Capturing attention is getting increasingly difficult in the channel surfing age. Getting full attention takes effort just shy of bringing Apollo 13 back to Earth.

Believe it or not, staff meetings can be an extraordinary opportunity. Let people have fun and they will enjoy attending. You might be thinking, "We don't have time for fun. This is their job and they shouldn't need a laser light show!" Well, what if that fun translates into a difference in your bottom line? What if the fun equals "message received"? When new procedures are not communicated properly, is there a cost associated with errors and repeated mistakes? You bet your bottom line there is.

Just to be clear, we are not suggesting you hire Robin Williams for your next meeting. His fees would negate all the extra profits his fun would bring in. There is a much more cost-efficient way to put fun into your meetings. The untapped talent is right in front of you. People in and around your office would love to "Spam it up" ("ham" is so overused). You will see a side of co-workers you never knew existed. Skits created to make a point about a new policy or procedure can make for a real attention-getter. To see a supervisor act out a part or to see the quiet person actually enjoying performing can have everyone enthralled.

Darren recently witnessed a parody of the TV game show *Jeopardy* at a major corporation. The contestants ranged from characters made up as Elvis to a man in drag. It is so easy to spoof movies, television programs, and current events. In the case of the *Jeopardy* parody, the point was to introduce a new program. The questions and answers were strategically created to illustrate key points. Those involved in creating the skit had fun. They put more effort into that presentation than if they had used a traditional style. The audience enjoyed watching, so the attention was intense. In the face of seeing co-workers and supervisors out of their element, the Oscar-worthiness of the performances meant little. In fact, it is probably better if the performances are poor, making it that much more amusing.

Do you think the points were remembered? Do you think the message was received? The morale of the presenters went up, too. Humor is easy in this type of atmosphere. It also helps in team-building. Where else could you use this idea?

RECAP:

- What are your staff meetings like now?
- What are the looks on people's faces on the way into these meetings?
- Are the presenters enthusiastic?
- How can you use this untapped "affordable" talent?
- Letting people have fun creates fun, and can help messages be clearer.
- How can you use this idea?

Ideas this gives you for your business:

CHAPTER 29

Make Wit,
Not War

A comedy secret to make
presentations interesting

---

*"Wit is the sudden marriage of ideas
which before their union were not
perceived to have any relation."*

– Mark Twain

The biggest myth about being funny is that you either "have it or you don't." No middle ground; it "cannot" be learned. Sure, some people have more natural talent than others, but being funny *can* be learned. Rick is a natural. At his first professional presentation he brought the house down, and it was a serious speech. It's the truth.

The program was designed to sell a software package he developed especially for retailers. Though Rick was a retail owner for 20 years and knew the business, he did not sell a single package. However, the audience absolutely loved him and a new career was born. Darren, on the other hand, was considered in high school "least likely to ever be funny." When he is playing a club locally and sees old friends and classmates, they think he is managing the club—until he takes the stage. The only time Darren's brother laughed is when Darren told him he was going to be a comedian.

Darren learned the hard way. He went to classes, read books (yes, they actually publish books about writing comedy material), and became a full-time student of comedy. He went to amateur nights week after week. Everyone in the comedy world told him the key is "stage time, stage time, stage time." Confidence and skill come primarily from on stage experience. Darren says that God did not give him the gift of laughter, God gave him the persistence to learn how. You can *learn* how funny people think.

Did you ever meet someone or see a comedian perform who you thought was spectacular? You were really impressed? Ever say to yourself, "I wish I was that witty. How do they do that?" One of the secrets of the stand-up comedy world is that the 5 minutes of material you see takes years and years of practice. If a comedian gets a spot on *The Tonight Show* or *Late Night*, the comic probably did the identical set every night for the past three weeks getting it perfect. Never mind the years it took to develop the persona and stage presence.

What is wit, anyway? Mark Twain says it perfectly in the quote that begins this chapter. How can you make wit? The same way witty people do! They relate things that we did not think were related before. There is a path that a funny person's mind follows. You can see on paper how it happens. A great way to demonstrate this and to use as a tool is by "making" an analogy. What would life be like without analogies? It would be like.... Thank goodness we have life with analogies. They help us understand foreign concepts by relating them to things we know.

When planning an important presentation we have a tendency to think to ourselves, "How can I make sure my listeners 'get it'? I want them to understand and remember. This is important stuff." If it is so important, why do we spend so much time on the concept and so little effort on making sure it is clear and remembered? If it is not clear and remembered, the effort on the concept or idea itself is wasted. Waste is no good for the bottom line.

The following exercise is taught in many stand-up comedy classes and books. Remember, your goal is to develop an analogy to make your point, process, or concept clearer and more memorable.

Take a piece of paper and make two columns plus a place for headings at the top of each. At the top of the right column put the title of your concept, process, or whatever it is you hope to impart to your audience. Darren did this once for a group of his colleagues. At the top of his right column he wrote "Professional Speaker."

	Professional Speaker

Next, in this column list everything possible related to the subject. If you spend less than 15 minutes vigorously writing even the most remote subjects that relate, you are not going deeply enough. It is the deepest ideas that make it the best. In our example, Darren came up with the following: personal story, microphone, introduction, nerves, first time, flip chart.

	Professional Speaker
	personal story
	microphone
	introduction
	nerves
	first time
	flip chart
	applause
	markers
	slides
	challenge
	motivating
	water
	the process
	knowledge
	love audiences

You must put time, effort, and thought into this exercise or it will not be very effective. It is incredibly helpful to have a partner. Your ideas will keep each other going deeper.

Now start the other column. Think wild. Think crazy. For its heading, choose something completely unrelated to your field of expertise. Make sure you don't pick anything that also appears in the right column. It is helpful to pick a "process" if what you are trying to describe is a process, or a policy if you are trying to talk about a new policy. If your topic is a process, try selecting another process, like "making a peanut butter sandwich." Think of something bizarre! The more bizarre the better…and the more memorable it will be.

If your concept is about growth, do not pick something stupid like growing a flower. Why is that stupid? It is too easy. It has been done! You would lose the memorable part. Remember Twain's "before their union [they] were not perceived to have any relation." If what you pick is already perceived to have a relation to your topic, it is not going to be as potent. For Darren's presentation to the speakers, he chose the 12-step programs.

12 Step Programs	Professional Speaker
	personal story
	microphone
	introduction
	nerves
	first time
	flip chart
	applause
	markers
	slides
	challenge
	motivating
	water
	the process
	knowledge
	love audiences

Once you have a heading on your left-hand column, brainstorm for anything and everything about that subject, with no regard for what you are trying to accomplish in the end. Do not skip a step. This is important! Take more time to develop this second list than the first. The first list you are familiar with, so expect the second to be tougher. Remember, the more ideas you have to choose from, the better this exercise will work and the more powerful your analogy will be. For his right column, Darren wrote down the following: coffee, friends, help, "hi, my name is," hall, meeting.

12 Step Programs	Professional Speaker
coffee	personal story
friends	microphone
help	introduction
"hi, my name is..."	nerves
hall	first time
meeting	flip chart
denial	applause
rehab	markers
nervous	slides
bright future	challenge
first time	motivating
admitting	water
responsibility	the process
addiction	knowledge
smoking	love audiences

After you have created a longer list under the left column, begin the next part. Scan the lists looking for similarities. Seek and ye shall find. The more you look, the more connections and similarities you will discover. Circle and connect the similar words and phrases. Then write these on a separate piece of paper across from each other, again in columns. Keep your original lists handy because you will find more similarities as you continue the process. From your new list of associations, write your presentation, as it should start to crystallize in front of you. Before he became a professional speaker Darren did this exercise with Humor and Native Americans as his column headers. He started at 11 at night and wrote his finished speech (word for word) at three in the morning for a 7:45 A.M. speech. It works.

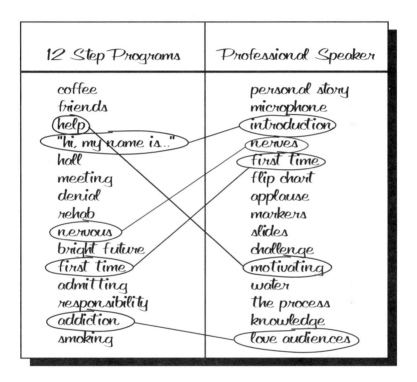

12 Step Programs	Professional Speaker
coffee	personal story
friends	microphone
help	introduction
"hi, my name is..."	nerves
hall	first time
meeting	flip chart
denial	applause
rehab	markers
nervous	slides
bright future	challenge
first time	motivating
admitting	water
responsibility	the process
addiction	knowledge
smoking	love audiences

Darren started his speech on the topic of professional speaking by describing what our speakers association is like. He began, "Hi, my name is Darren and I am a Speak-o-holic." Does this stuff work? He got to speak at our national convention in one year with the same speech. Because he is incredible? No, because it was a sudden marriage of ideas which, before their union, were not perceived to have any relation. That is why people loved it.

Darren showed this process and concept to Mark, a marketing manager for a major corporation. He watched as Mark presented his version of the marketing department's strategy to the division where he worked. He started his overheads with a slide that said "Gone Fishin' (Be back in three years)." He covered the strategy for three years in a delightful and entertaining way. Most important, it was clearly understood.

If you do it right but your analogy does not end up funny, it will still be interesting. You are not expected to be funny, so there is a lot less pressure on you than on a comedian. You are making a point. If you relate a process of yours to creating a peanut butter sandwich, do you think they will remember it? You might even find one on your desk the next morning.

This tool is simple, but it does take effort, thought, and time. Time is important, but isn't your message worth taking the time to make it remembered?

RECAP:

- Do the exercise.
- Remember the depth of the lists is key.
- Try it—you'll like it.

Ideas this gives you for your business:

_____

_____

_____

_____

_____

_____

_____

_____

_____

_____

_____

_____

CHAPTER 30

The 3 Most Powerful Questions

Do you have the guts to ask them?

"Seek and ye shall find."

– The Holy Bible

I n an article by Alix Nyberg in the *Boston Globe's* web publication, BusinessToday.com, Sarah Drummey, Human Resource Manager at The Sheraton Harborside Portsmouth, says, "LaCroix's ideas helped the hotel revolutionize the way it ran meetings." This success came from asking only three questions and making the most of the answers.

Whoa—sounds like this chapter is going to be deep. We always want things to be simple and easy. They never seem to be. If people find an easy method, we think it cannot be any good. It cannot possibly have any value. Human nature is funny that way. Who says God does not have a sense of humor? The three questions we present to you in this chapter are simple and basic. They are easy to ask and extremely difficult to answer if you choose to seek the *true* answers. Why? Because they are not normal business-type questions. We do not usually ask them in the boardroom or in our own minds.

Most agree that at its core, business is built on relationships. If you cannot look at these questions as important business questions, look at them as relationship-building questions. If you have trouble answering them, ask a child under 10. No, they do not understand business because they major in fun. Oops, the secret is out. Kids can help break your tunnel vision. Listen, really listen to them and their answers. (Oh, and by the way, these questions do work in your personal and family life, too.)

Question #1 –
How can you relieve your own tension?

What? What does that mean? How do I relieve my own tension? It's the Oxygen Principle on an airplane. What do they tell you to do if the cabin loses pressure and the oxygen masks fall? Usually they tell you to put on your own mask first and then assist any children near you. Why? Because you cannot help them if you are dead or can't breathe! With your own mask on you will be in much better shape to assist others. It is the same thing with tension. Start with yourself.

First you have to notice when you are frustrated. How do you know when you are uptight? How do you act? What do you do? Throw things? If you are like Darren, a cute little vein pops out on the side of your forehead. (You can see it in some of his television commercials.) We all know the signs in others. If you don't know your own ask those close to you. They will be happy to tell you. You might be surprised at what you aren't aware of. And you want to be aware of signals indicating that you aren't at the top of your game, or—worse yet—a liability to your end goal.

Once you know you are stressed, what are you going to do about it? What is your plan? We plan everything else, from meetings to budgets, so why not your own answer to being stressed? Combat it ahead of time when you are thinking clearly. What calms your savage breast, or cracks you up? Is it a certain type of music, silly pictures of your kids, or a favorite comedian? If it's a favorite comedian, why not have an emergency recording with you labeled, "open in case of tension." It can be played in your car or through headphones on a portable player.

Our environment has a major influence on us. Have you taken a good look at your environment lately? What do you keep handy to battle the inevitable tensions of work and life? Make a plan just for the health of it. If that is not enough motivation, how about the fact that such a plan can help you be more effective? Do you want to be more effective? Are you willing to try something different? Make a plan.

Question #2 –
How can you relieve the tension of others?

If, in fact, business is about relationships, we should consider the tensions of those around us. If we can help them relieve their own tensions, we can build stronger bonds with them. This goes for internal as well as external customers. Some of the basics can be quite easy—just ask anyone who works in the front lines of customer service. If it is a repetitive job, a little creative brainstorming can help relieve the tension of an unavoidable occurrence. A little lightheartedness can send a message to the customer saying, "Hey, we understand how you feel, we are sorry, and we cared enough about you and your business to do something about it." Isn't that what customers want—more understanding? There are three kinds of customers to think about in this question, existing customers, new customers, and internal customers.

Existing customers:

Regular clients are a financial necessity. In the course of normal business, problems will inevitably arise. If you have a good relationship with customers caught up in one of these problem "situations," they probably will not take their business elsewhere, even though, in their mind, your company might have lost a couple of goodwill points. Goodwill is especially important in the age of exceptional customer service.

What are some of your company's recurring frustrations — from your customer's point of view? One unavoidable frustration that Darren came across affects a company called Cape Air. When he spoke with those in customer service, it became apparent that a recurring problem is fog. That's right, fog! Cape Air is a community-oriented regional airline. It flies passengers around Cape Cod and the islands of Massachusetts. One of their customers' most common frustrations is the fog. Clients ask, "When is it going to lift so we can depart?" Some even go so far as to ask, "How long have you worked here? And you cannot tell me when it is going to lift?" (The patient customer representatives are not meteorologists.) If clients are on a tight schedule they are even more uptight, but nothing can be done. Nothing about the fog, that is.

What would you do? How would you relieve a delayed customer's tension? You can concentrate on the problem or on the tension. Obviously, if the problem can be rectified it should come first. Humor is not the be-all and the end-all. It is a means to a stronger business and better client relationships. But if the problem cannot be rectified....

Daniel Wolf, president of Cape Air, has developed an environment in which creative solutions are encouraged. When Darren spoke to this group, the first idea that popped into his head was to put up a sign along the lines of:

Our direct phone line to God is temporarily disconnected.
We are unsure when the fog will lift.

What the representatives actually did was to make a fun game of it. They took guesses from the waiting customers. Sounds to us like a combination of Wait Management and Inclusionary Humor! They made the fun interactive. The best part was that employees of Cape Air were encouraged to come up with the solution themselves. They were not told what to do in order to have fun; they were just given permission to do it.

New customers:

Sometimes getting a new client can be a seemingly insurmountable challenge. How can you be different? How can you get a prospective client's attention? How can you start the relationship off on the right foot? Can you guess what our answer might be? Duh!

One of the problems that we encounter as humor consultants is being taken seriously by people who are caught up in the traditional business mindset. Traditional is great unless you are trying to sell an untraditional idea.

One of Darren's goals was to teach at his alma mater, the Bryant College Center for Management Development. The person in charge of programming at the time was Barbara. During the course of their conversations it became obvious to Darren that Barbara had a great sense of humor, but she also had a deadline approaching that was haunting her. This was a source of tension—something to stay away from during a sales call—but it can also be an opportunity. If you can help someone to laugh at tension you are also giving them energy and power to battle it. This is customer service at its finest!

Knowing Barbara had a sense of humor, Darren decided to shake things up a bit, especially since he didn't seem to be making much progress with the sell. He decided to key in on the deadline. Hey, this is what he teaches and believes in. It's time to put it into action. It's time for what Darren calls Humor by Mail! Tah dah! Making someone laugh without even being there is powerful and fun.

It is very helpful to know the prospective client as well as possible. Such information can be incredibly valuable when coming up with ideas. It also shows you were listening and you care. Barbara had things around her office to help her keep her sense of humor in tough times. What could Darren get for her that would actually make an impact?

He found a 12-inch aspirin, an authentic replica of a real aspirin, but it was HUGE! (Just a note: stay away from cheesy items even if you want to make a less-expensive point. Go first class or don't do it at all. Cheesy things look just that—cheap. This is a reflection of you. Spend the money, it's an investment in a future client. Besides, why would you want to look anything but first rate?) Darren sent off the huge aspirin with a note that read, "Hope this helps you to keep your sense of humor as you approach the stressful deadline." That is it. He let the rest happen on its own.

After a week of not hearing anything, he was dying to call and see what she thought. In another couple of days he received a letter. Barbara wrote that she loved the aspirin, but she did him one better. She started a "Headache of the Day" in her office. Think about that. The huge aspirin traveled from desk to desk around the office. Whoever was having a tough day got to have the aspirin sit there to help them and to let those around them into their mindset. How do you think someone in that office who was obviously stressed would react if someone else came over and put the aspirin on his or her desk? Our guess is that a big smile would result. The stressed individual would feel good about the person who noticed and was trying to help.

An added bonus is that Darren's contact information is subtly printed on the aspirin. Now people he never met are getting to know who he is and what he does. Who do you think they might call the next time they are looking for a speaker?

We love it when people take our ideas and one-up us! Can you? It might just improve your bottom line! Where could you use the Humor by Mail concept? Oh, and by the way…Darren became the youngest person to teach for the Center for Management Development. Was it just because of the aspirin? No! Did it help? Barbara still keeps in contact though she has moved on to her own business.

Internal customers:

Darren was presenting to a woman's business group. As he usually does, he was opening their minds to the practical use of humor as a business problem solver. That's right, problem solver! As he led the group through the exercises, the participants laughed and came up with silly ideas that they threw out to one another. In a fun environment, people are more open about their thoughts and more open for brainstorming. This is the best kind of circumstance.

Darren said he will never forget one participant's calling him up after the program, totally elated about an idea that was generated during the session. Her problem had to do with the mailroom. Evidently, the mailroom staff was having a difficult time remembering where a certain department's mail was to go. It was consistently sent to an incorrect mail stop within the company. The departments had tried desperately to straighten the problem out through conventional methods. Frustration mounted as time went on. Haven't we all been through situations within a company where the solution seems so obvious to us, but our politically correct hands are tied?

The participant, who was open to anything that would work, had a thought hit her during the humor session. What she came up with was giving the gift of a huge jar of jellybeans to the mailroom, with the department's name and mail stop permanently marked on the side of the jar. Why huge? So it would stand out, be looked at regularly, and last a long time. By the time the staff finished the jellybeans, the new habit would be formed and correct information would be communicated. This was all accomplished with a gift, one having positive connotations rather than negative reprimands. The smile on the participant's face told the story of another problem solved through humor!

Question #3 (the most powerful) – How can we make this fun?

That's right, the question seems simple at first glance, but there's gold in that thar question. It's a process question. When you start to think about the far-reaching effects of humorizing, or of making the most mundane jobs fun, and even of making the creation of fun competitive, you see that you can accomplish anything for your business. In a *Wall Street Journal* article, Hal Lancaster wrote about a restaurant chain called McGuffey's. Twenty percent of the manager's raise depends on how much fun he or she is to work with. Keith Dunn, president of the company, was quoted as saying, "Results are still the primary goal, we're in a service business with a high turnover. It's part of the manager's job to bring fun to the workplace." The key to all of this is—it starts with the simple question of how can we make this fun?

The Sheraton Harborside in Portsmouth, New Hampshire, wanted to do something different. Sarah Drummey, who was in charge of Human Resources, and Shari Young, now the General Manager of the hotel, asked Darren to deliver a program on customer service for an employee rally. The program was to kick off the new year. Darren was chosen over some customer service gurus because of his background as a comedian. They wanted their message delivered in a fun, upbeat, and entertaining manner that would make the message stick!

The most powerful part of the assignment was the initial meeting with the management staff because they were totally open to ideas. They told Darren that the goal was to present the message "Whatever it Takes," and to empower the employees to resolve as many situations as they could using their own judgment. Management wanted its employees to make decisions on the spot. Darren came up with the idea of centering the meeting around the popular football advertising spot, "You Make the Call." Shari and the management staff loved the idea and ran with it.

As for the supervisory staff, Darren's initial meeting proved to be less than enthusiastic, especially since management was trying to maintain some confidentiality about the theme. The management staff recognized the reluctance of the supervisors and decided they had to take action to get the supervisors to buy into the idea. They made a brilliant call by deciding to get the supervisors involved. All the supervisors received football jerseys, making them part of the event without full disclosure. Their enthusiasm soon spread. The employees were kept totally in the dark about the employee rally. All they knew was that the meeting was mandatory! This set up a wonderfully inviting atmosphere of surprise. Expecting a boring meeting, the employees were blown away when they walked in the door. Talk about atmosphere! It was a speaker's dream. The management staff went beyond Darren's expectations, as well. When they decorated the function room, they pulled out all the stops. A beer distributor had been contacted for decorations and they came through. Blimps hung from the ceiling, streamers hung in the doorway, posters covered the walls, goal posts were in place, and astro-turf covered the floor. To take it a step further, the supervisors were passing out popcorn and soda, stadium music was blaring from the sound system, and cheerleaders with pompons cheered!

Then it was game time! The looks on the faces of the employees as they came in the door said it all. They knew right away this was going to be different. Do you think they were more open to listening at this point than they had been 5 minutes earlier when they walked down the hall thinking about another mandatory meeting? Already it was more memorable than any meeting ever before. Although the normal status reports, facts, and updates were presented, they were done in a lively way. The management staff became the commentators and statisticians. The owner of the hotel made an inspirational speech in the role of the football commissioner. Two of the male managers played the role of the cheerleaders, adding a certain punch to the program. Darren wrapped up the meeting with his customer service program, doing so in the role of the referee.

Everyone—from the owner to the employees to the management staff—enjoyed themselves. After the program, Darren spoke to one of the attendees and asked, "What did you like best?" The participant thought a moment and replied with certainty, "It was great to see the managers up there having fun; we always see them uptight." What a powerful statement! The managers were now perceived as real people! Humor bonds, and in this case it bonded the employees with management. It focused employees away from high tension areas of work to a team-building experience—a coming together. As we stated earlier, "People we laugh with, we tend to trust." Where did it all stem from? The open minds of the management staff and the question, "How can we make this fun?"

RECAP:

- How can you relieve your own tension? What is your plan? Don't have one? Make one!

- How can you relieve the tension of others? Locating their tension could just be the key to stronger relationships.

- Ask the question "How can we make it fun?" What is it? Any aspect of your business you want to improve!

- The unexpected can be a powerful tool of wonderment.

- Humor converts the mundane and mandatory into an "EVENT."

- The hidden benefit is that humor raises the bar for effective and entertaining meetings for the future.

- The buy-in of management and supervisors uses the "Inclusionary Factor" that creates a team effect.

- Project the image of an enlightened management team.

- Having a fun meeting decreases turnover, increases employee loyalty, and attracts quality people.

- Employees work harder for "people" than they do for "suits."

Ideas this gives you for your business:

_____

_____

_____

_____

CHAPTER 31

The Cannoli Principle

A message is more digestible when delivered with humor

---

*"If an idea doesn't have a bit of absurdity,
then it has no merit."*

– Albert Einstein

Recently, Darren had a rather unusual speaking (if you'd call it that) assignment. He, along with his colleague Robert Siciliano, worked a movie theater for the sole purpose of hyping a new feature unique to conventional movie cinemas. It was an amusement park "ride simulator," an apparatus to make the seats move with the action on the screen. For some reason, the management of the theater wanted to do something different. They faced the unique challenge of promoting this feature when no advertising could be done.

The theater was previewing this simulator, we'll call *The Ride,* before all of its regularly scheduled movies, as if it were just another preview for an upcoming film. But only 2 to 3 percent of the theatre patrons were purchasing tickets for this unique movie experience. Management didn't feel *The Ride*'s full potential was being tapped. They believed it needed something more. With percentages that low they were often forced to run *The Ride,* bearing the cost of an operator, while having only three or four people in the theater. Not the most cost-effective way of doing business! Not to mention that with such a small attendance the excitement of the ride was missing—the roars and screams of the crowd.

Elaine, general manager for the cinema, had a dream about how to promote *The Ride.* She thought it would be extremely effective to have live characters experiencing *The Ride* in front of the captive audiences before each regular movie. Yes, pitchmen. However, she did not want a hit-em'-over-the-head type of sales approach because it would turn off the patrons. She contacted Darren's agent, Rhonda Flashing, who suggested to Elaine an interactive improvisational humor format. Get the audience involved and let them have a good time. After all, why does someone go to a movie? To be entertained and have a good time!

Rhonda was, of course, aware of Darren's comedy background and his experience in the "Improv Wedding Shows." He was a natural choice, along with Robert Siciliano, also a seasoned veteran of the wedding shows. Darren and Robert became known as The Cannoli Brothers, Joey and Tony. These two guys were fun-loving, loud, a little obnoxious (though not offensive), but highly effective salespeople. Their goal was to sell tickets to *The Ride,* and that is exactly what these two lovable buffoons did. They broke all records for admission to it. Attendance jumped 600 to 1000 percent. Upwards of 20 percent of the patrons were going to see *The Ride* on the weekends the Cannoli Brothers were performing.

Did Darren and Robert go to that theater to be salesmen? No! They went to perform. They were hired not because they had any great selling skills, but because they possess a talent to perform and the ability to interact with an audience to make their experience fun! They went to have a good time. If you ask either of them they will tell you about the fun they had.

Another major benefit occurred that wasn't anticipated, but it reaped wonderful rewards. The employees were having a ball with the entire experience. They could not wait for the return of the Cannoli Brothers. As one employee put it, "It wasn't even like working today, we just had so much fun." They even took pictures of the Cannoli Brothers and put the pictures up in the employee lounge to remind them of the fun they had. All they have to do is look at those pictures to put them in a good mood. (Hey, it's the Clown Principle again!)

Don't you want your company's employees to say that every day? It can be achieved by simply shifting the way you think about humor and remembering how you can HUMORIZE a project.

For all the doubting Thomases out there, the bottom line was the bottom line. Yes, they had to pay Darren and Robert, but the theater made MONEY and created product awareness like never before. In one weekend 30,000 people saw the Cannoli Brothers perform. No one said, "Look, these guys are trying to sell us." They did say, "Hey, that's funny," or "That was different." What do people say or think after your sales presentation? Some of the management at the cinema didn't jump on the bandwagon until the results were in. Now they are believers. (We can't mention any names to protect the guilty.) The act was "the sales pitch that got applause."

RECAP:

- Humor sells.

- The way we approach our job can determine its outcome. Make it fun.

- Creative humorous solutions begin with asking some questions that might sound a little different.

- How many sales pitches have you ever heard end with applause? (Now you know of at least one).

- Creativity is the key, not always money investment. (Inclusionary humor can be more memorable than a million-dollar budget.)

- Happy employees create a fun attitude that keeps the customer coming back.

- The bottom line is the bottom line.

Ideas this gives you for your business:

_____

_____

_____

_____

_____

_____

_____

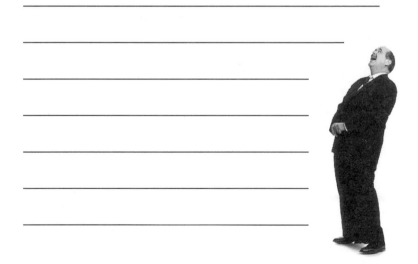

CHAPTER 32

Make Your Event the Specialest

Be remembered

"The comedy situation arises from the incongruity between a certain character and the situation in which the character finds himself."

– Jack Benny, *Sunday Nights at Seven*

Yes, Rick and Darren know that "specialest" is not really a word. They think it should be. It is easier than saying "the most special," and it got your attention. People love to correct other people. In Darren's comedy act he usually says, after putting himself down with humble humor about being Polish, *"Well what did you expect for an eight-dollar cover charge?"* The cover charge is more. Someone in the audience always corrects him, falling right into his trap. *"Ten dollars, wow! I guess this Polish joke would be on you then!"*

When Darren started writing comedy he went to learn it from a man named Stanley Ralph Ross. Stan is an accomplished comedy writer in Hollywood, his experience ranging from episodes of *All In the Family* to some of the award-winning episodes of *Cosby*. Stan used the word "mostest." He opened Darren's eyes to the fact that all of our favorite characters on TV stand out for one reason or another. Whatever their quirk is, it is exaggerated so that it stands out. Idiots are the biggest idiots, the dumb are the dumbest, and the lazy are the laziest. This is not just the case in comedy—it is true for dramatic characters, too.

What does this have to do with special events? Everything! Are your events really "special" or are they the same old things you do every year, just with a new theme? What is new or different about your special event this year? If it is annual and not significantly different from last year's, what should we call it? How about an unevent? What do the people who get to attend it feel, "special"?

Yes, we are overusing the word "special" in this chapter because it is overused in the corporate world, thereby diluting its meaning. So, special ain't so special any more. Introducing... the new word the "specialest"! Tah dah!

Want an example? How about a golf tournament? How can you make this special event the specialest? There is a chain of convenience stores in New England that holds an annual golf tournament for its vendors. They wanted to make the next year's the "specialest." Well, the Cannoli Brothers strike again, only this time they brought "their mom"! This unhappy dysfunctional family took to the golf course, thanks again to Rhonda, their agent. What did they do? They played a little golf, drove around in the cart arguing, and entertained all day. They became "the humor detour."

The Cannoli family posed as new, clueless vendors, so excited to be at this prestigious country club, being taken such good care of. They hoarded all of the free stuff they could. The boys went to try their luck fishing (wearing full gear in the water hazard), and Mom hung her bloomers out to dry on the ninth hole strung between two golf carts for all to see. Mama also put on her bathing suit to sun herself while she brought cold drinks to some of the golfers. Many people did not know what to make of them. Darren did not know what to make of the Cannoli family either.

This was an event that will be remembered for a long time. Next time those vendors go golfing we are sure they will still have a little chuckle when they remember the event that included the Cannoli Family. It was the "specialest" event. Someone planned it, and someone had the guts to break out of the box. The bar was not raised at this event, it was retired!

RECAP:

- "Specialest" is now a word! Add it to your vocabulary and your spell checker.
- What are your special events?
- How can you make them "specialest?"
- What could be incongruous there? Incongruity = humor potential!

Ideas this gives you for your business:

PART IV

PEOPLE WHO USE THE TOOLS

CHAPTER 33

Are You Having Fun Yet?

The Script

"Laugh at your problems,
everybody else does."

– Unknown

S it back and enjoy this chapter. It is the script to a free recording Rick sent out to large retailers who expressed interest in him. Now is a good time for reviewing all we have learned and seeing how those points were used in an actual marketing piece. Remember, this was sent only to large retailers:

"The times they are a-changing." How many times have you heard that line? They are always changing, but are you? The days of having employees and beating them into submission, knowing they would never leave their jobs, are OVER! (They were very good years, but you just can't do that stuff any more.) Remember when they were just happy to get a paycheck? Not any more!

Now employees talk about quality time. It used to mean working 14-hour days, but now they have other interests that are more important than the job. (I find this hard to accept as well, but the times, they are a-changing.)

We have Generation X-ers out there that everyone is trying to figure out but can't, 'cause they are still trying to "find themselves." They think differently than we do and have different values. Scary, huh?

The same old ways of motivating people just don't work any more. Now, if that isn't bad enough, we have customers who want it all, as well. The reason is simple. The competition is so keen, it has created some companies that give exceptional customer service as the ultimate corporate differentiater. Then there are other companies that are willing to just give it all away. And what do we do? We match their price. Why should they lose money alone? Misery loves company.

It's the things that separate us, as business people, that I am talking about. Too many times the only thing that separates businesses is price. We are selling commodities, and we don't know anyone who has ever made money in commodities other than some guy on an infomercial that runs at 2:30 A.M. in Dubuque. Even the great Wal-Mart is not only advertising falling prices, but also showing that nice little lady with the winning smile who says, "Welcome to Wal-Mart." (How do they get them to smile all the time? Let's be honest, don't you sometimes feel like saying, "Wipe that smile off your face and stop laughing and be miserable like the rest of us!"?)

How do you think a retailer feels when a customer comes into the store and asks, "Why don't you carry a certain line any more?" The customer tells you how much she loved it and is so disappointed in you for no longer carrying it. You feel like saying, "Ma'am, you were the only one in America who bought that line. If I kept on carrying it, I would be out of business." But we can't say things like that. After all, we are business people. We have to be more diplomatic.

Have you ever had an employee come up to you and ask, "How come she got more hours this week than I did?" You feel like saying it's because you like her more, but we can't say that!

Don't we love it when a customer asks us why something is so expensive? You feel like saying it's because you want to make a lot of money and retire to Arizona. But we can't say that, either. We are constantly thinking things we can't say.

So are you having fun yet? Has the fun left your business because of some tough years? Or maybe we are remembering those years through rose-colored glasses.

The reason I named this tape "Are You Having Fun Yet" is because I hear that line every time I go out to speak. There is always someone saying, "It just isn't fun any more," but then I find some retailers having the time of their lives. The strange thing about it is they just happen to be the same retailers who are winning awards at the annual mall meetings for beating out other stores. Many times they are even independents beating out the major stores.

A year ago Rick spoke in Chambersburg, Pennsylvania. The Number 1 store in the mall (per square-foot of sales and percent of increase) was Musselman Jewelers. Has anyone ever heard of Musselman Jewelers? This is not a commonly known name in the retail business, yet they beat all the biggies. There is no reason they should be winning, but they do.

It's about doing business in the '90s and beyond; it's about a tool right under our noses that keeps customers, keeps employees, and even helps our bottom line. We're talking about the strategic use of humor in our businesses, in our management, and in every aspect you can possibly think of. When was the last time we reviewed what we were doing and asked the question: How can we humorize it? We're not talking about a program today or tomorrow; we're talking about changing our corporate culture to create the humor environment.

When do you get your best ideas? Better yet, when do you think? Either on the john or in the shower. Basically, when you are relaxed. That's just one of the benefits from a humor environment: ideas flow, and it's much better than putting showers and toilets in all the offices.

See, we believe in what we call the Balloon Theory. When things are light, sales and productivity go up. It's time to put that smile on our faces and start laughing—our sales will go up and our turnover will go down. We just don't accomplish as much when we are uptight or stressed. Humor is the helium of life and the great separator of businesses.

Remember one key element we often forget: our customers aren't working. They come into our stores to relieve their stresses by buying something new, and how do we make them feel? We say things like "it's over there" or "all we have is out" or even "the store is closing in five minutes so hurry up." That's not the way to make people happy.

Did you ever notice that when a new manager takes over a store, sometimes sales just go up for no apparent reason other than the new person's attitude is more upbeat or looser? It's not that they make extra sales, it's just that they don't prevent sales from happening. They create a fun feeling or a humor-generating environment. Sometimes their paperwork might not be up to the old manager's standard but they can reassign some of that work to an assistant for the sake of the sales increases.

It hit Rick one day at a mall after speaking at a sister mall. Here was an identical store in an almost identical mall with similar demographics, but the two stores were having very different sales results. One manager was upbeat and perky and the other was very serious and very corporate and businesslike. When are we going to realize that fun and the use of humor sells? The upbeat and perky manager won all the awards but was still humble, while the corporate manager maintained a stand-offish demeanor. She couldn't be bothered with small talk. Sorry! This is a business of small talk and attitudes.

We are in the entertainment business! We don't need to know more ways to mark things down so that the consumer thinks it's a lot but we really know it isn't. Our goal is rather elementary, but works almost every time. Let your customers have a good time when they shop, and laugh your way to the bank.

It works!

RECAP:

- This tape was a highly successful marketing tape that received much attention and worked. It brought in business.

- Why do you think it was so effective?

- What ideas does this give you?

Ideas this gives you for your business:

CHAPTER 34

The Laughter in the Dough

Watch the bottom line rise

---

*"If you don't have fun then
shut the damn thing down."*

- Fitzroy Alexander

One of the fastest rising companies in New England has a secret ingredient baked into its organization which enables it to make a lot of dough.

It took us only 30 minutes to write that opening line. We had so much to work with that we got confused by so many potential puns, and that's the yeast we could do. "Enough with the play on words!" Rick is yelling to Darren. "Alright," Darren says, "we'll keep the rest of the chapter unleavened." (Not bad for a Catholic.) Rick thinks that Darren is going off a little half-baked.

What we are writing about is a company that isn't half-baked, but three-quarters baked. The company is Signature Breads of Somerville, Massachusetts, specialists in Par-Baked Bread. For those of you who are not familiar with par-baking, don't feel bad, Rick wasn't either until he toured the company.

Par-baking is baking the bread to 70 percent of completion, freezing it, and shipping the product frozen. The end user finishes the baking process for the ultimate in freshness and short bake time eliminates waste. This 5-year-old company went from $60,000 in sales its first year to over $20 million, and that's a lot of dough. This company works three shifts a day and is in the process of moving its facility to a much larger plant in Medford, a neighboring town.

You can pick up any business publication to read about success stories like this one, but what surprised us was how and why this company did what it did.

Before we begin, let us say that originally we had no intention of having the following interview end up on these pages. Rick was doing some freelance writing for a business newsletter and was asked to interview and write a story about Signature Breads. He made a number of calls to get the appointment and finally gave up, telling his editor he just could not catch this gentleman named Fitzroy Alexander. The editor started calling until he got Rick the appointment.

Rick didn't expect much when he walked into this commercial bakery in a very industrial part of town, but then the "Wows" began. When Rick asked for his secret to success, Fitzroy was quick to say that the Number 1 factor is quality. The way he gets his people to think quality is by making the corporate culture one that cares about people and the product. Okay, we have all heard that before. But what separates Signature from the rest of the world is that its attitude and use of humor is intertwined throughout the culture of the organization. Alexander stood up and said, "If you don't have fun then shut the damn thing down." Rick believes he absolutely meant it.

During the interview, Alexander kept getting calls and interruptions, and he always had a smile, a joke, or a laugh. Everyone who interrupted had that same loose type of attitude. Alexander went on to say that humor is the company's way of expressing a caring attitude about its people. We care, so we make it fun for them to be here. They don't want to leave because it is enjoyable for them to work here and they like us.

We have all heard about respecting an employer, but liking is very, very helpful, and in the long run, cost-effective. So much for high turnover!

The interesting part about Signature is that the make-up of the employees would ordinarily be classified as a difficult type of work force. Alexander employs 90 people from 15 countries, and they are mostly all hourly personnel. He has many employees who come to him without being able to speak a word of English. He introduced Rick to one of his supervisors, who was laughing and joking with them. Alexander told Rick that four years earlier, when the supervisor was hired, he could not speak a word of English. You can't even say that someone's speaking Spanish is an advantage because so many people are of different origins. The most common language is English.

One of the biggest challenges that Alexander had with his fun philosophy was the varied background of his employees. Laughter was simply not part of their cultures. With so many diverse cultures and having to cope with so many immigrants, laughter had to be *taught*. It wasn't as natural as one might expect. (And you thought laughter would be tough to bring to *your* company?) These people had not been exposed to employers who welcomed fun and recreation as a means to productivity. Isn't this the same challenge that faces corporate America: the acceptance and encouragement of humor as a productivity tool?

Alexander made an interesting analogy. He said, "The reason to have fun is because everyone is interested in the end result." Rick was a little confused over that one. He questioned further. Alexander said that everyone has a customer. The person who makes the dough has to satisfy the person who puts it into the machine that creates the different shapes and types of bread. That person has to satisfy the person who puts the bread into the refrigerator to ferment for 16 hours. That person must then satisfy the person who rolls the bread into the ovens, and that person must satisfy the person who rolls it into the freezer, and that person must satisfy the packer who has the toughest job of all in having to satisfy the ultimate customer!

By using humor and fun techniques, rapport is increased, which in turn makes a positive impact on productivity. A side benefit of this type of positive environment is that it fosters process improvement ideas. Those positive ideas affect the bottom line and the quality that Alexander holds as his top priority.

RECAP:

- Humor in business is not a half-baked idea — or 3/4. It's people who believe that humor does not belong who are half-baked. Help them rise to their full potential—give them this book!

- If fun and humor can be a "bridge over cultures" and are the common ingredients in productivity at Signature, why are they not being tapped fully at your company? Who is blocking it? What can you do about it? What will you do about it?

- If productivity and turnover mean nothing to you, neither will this chapter!

- What else do you get out of this chapter?

- Go ahead—just try to argue with Fitzroy's success!

Ideas this gives you for your business:

_____

_____

_____

_____

_____

_____

_____

CHAPTER 35

And This Little Piggy Built a Business

The power of the pig

"Through pastry and persistence all things are possible."

– Mac the Pig

In our search to seek out the most lucrative and powerful applications of humor, Darren stumbled onto a talking pig named Mac. Stop! It's not what you are thinking, but the word "pig" may have just peaked your interest enough to read on. That is what good humor does. It breaks the thinking pattern and creates interest.

Where did Darren first fall in love with this pig? For starters it wasn't at a barnyard dance or even a sleazy singles bar. It was when Darren was speaking at a "Woman in Business" function. He had arrived at the meeting site early to set up for his presentation. While setting up, he was alone with Rita Schiano, one of the proprietors of the Casual Café in Sturbridge, Massachusetts. Then Darren noticed that a pink plaster of Paris pig was watching him.

He immediately started to talk to Rita about the pig. Poof! He had just become a victim of Mac the pig. He had succumbed to the "Power of the Pig." That is a *real* power-Mac (sorry PC users). Mac gave the conversation a boost and made communication easier by presenting an interesting subject.

This is a talking pig that worked his magical power without even saying a word. Darren found out that Mac usually has a lot to say. He also has an attitude! His thoughts of the day are communicated via a chalkboard. What Rita and Karen, her partner, have created is this third party icon that lets them say things they cannot, breaks the ice with new customers, and creates conversation with the established clientele. Mac has taken on a personality of his own, which helps cement relationships with the customers (like Mickey does for Disney).

Rita and Karen try to make Mac's comments clever, timely, and somewhat philosophical. When *The Silence of the Lambs* won an Oscar, the message read, "Have a friend for dinner." During the brouhaha over Clinton's pot smoking statement, Mac wore a saxophone and the board said, "Smoked hams don't inhale."

Some of the classics from Mac are, "Through pastry and persistence all things are possible," and on Valentine's Day, "Be mine you swine!" On Mother's Day Mac said, "Remember Mother's Day or you will be sow-ry." On Easter, Mac pleaded for his fellow pigs when he said, "Eat lamb, not ham." Along with the holiday themes, politics are generously sprinkled in, like when he said, "Hillary rodHAM Clinton—now that is Porkfection."

Mac's views are not necessarily the views and opinions of the management. That is a great disclaimer for any people who might take offense. It makes it easy to just blame the pig. Mac becomes the safe "fall guy." His feelings are never hurt. He never wants a raise. He doesn't need medical insurance or even a 401(k) plan. He just spreads his goodwill and clever ideas throughout all the hours the restaurant is open.

The power of Mac lies in breaking the ice between the restaurant's owners and their customers. He transforms the customers from casual observers to loyal and dedicated customers. How loyal are they? How many of your customers send your co-workers postcards from all over the world? Not to mention the gifts he gets at Christmas. Four customers even sent Mac pairs of sunglasses, one of which was valued at over $100. That is respect!

The Casual Café has taken things a step further and started a Mac slogan contest. The first year it had to be canceled due to lack of participation. Rita and Karen did not give up. Incorporating humor into organizations takes time but eventually becomes an integral part of the business. Though it took a while to catch on, each year more and more people try their hand at putting words into Mac's mouth. The contestants are the customers who have gotten to know him. Once they are involved, the bond gets tighter, (It's that inclusionary humor in action again.) The winners receive dinner for two at the Café, and—more important—recognition for officially making Mac speak. The worst saying or pun submitted receives small change to buy a Big Mac at McDonald's. Rita and Karen now believe this "less-than-silent partner" has become a powerful asset.

RECAP:

- Humor breaks the thinking pattern, train of thought, and "the ice" with new customers.
- Humor creates curiosity and interest.
- A disclaimer takes the ownership of the comment away from the establishment and makes the pig the "fall guy." Who is your pig?
- Icons work around the clock, serve goodwill, and break the ice for NO pay. Sometimes they have to be dusted.
- Well-placed humor such as Mac can transform customers from casual observers into loyal patrons.

- What type of icon could work for your company or department? If it sounds dumb, remember everyone had an imaginary friend at one time or another.
- Humor can take time to develop, but it will have a lasting and far-reaching effect.
- A humor icon is a powerful "silent" partner. It can also become a lovable "mascot" for a department. How can you use this idea?

Ideas this gives you for your business:

_____

_____

_____

_____

_____

_____

CHAPTER 36

Negotiating Humor Homework

Dr. Roger Andersen, President of The Devry Institute of Technology

---

"The shortest distance between two people is a laugh."

– Victor Borge

WOW!! Darren is yelling at me to write, but I can't. We just got blown away by an interview with a little-known but soon to be famous college president of The Devry Institute of Technology. He is the author of the book *Some Days You're the Pigeon and Some Days You're the Statue.* Does he believe in the use of humor by a college president? Yes, but more than that, he lives it, eats it, and drinks it. Humor is the very essence of his life. Because it's just a cool thing to do? No! Because it gets results. He has converted a conservative campus doing things the traditional way into a place where people want to work because it is not only professional but also fun.

Dr. Andersen stated that now is the worst of times to start to introduce the message of humor into a company because this is the most turbulent time for business, due to downsizing, restructuring, and outsourcing. Unfortunately, humor is not a part of the higher pecking order of must-save resources. However, he went on to say, these are really the best of times to humorize your organization or environment because you are dealing with greater roles for employees and employee empowerment. Downsizing and restructuring create a fertile environment for the value of humor to be recognized as an alternative tool to help companies get through periods of transition. Added responsibilities for employees and morale problems start to become major distractions. Humor allows us to be able to deal with serious issues in a lighter, more productive way.

He summed it all up by stressing that "trying to incorporate humor into firms at this time would be appropriate to counteract the impacts from the structural changes that are occurring. So I hope it would happen that more businesses consider humor, and they will when it is in the best interest, financially, for the company, which means absolutely nothing. If you have a CEO who is inclined to adopt a humor policy it will happen. If you don't, they use the budget excuse."

Thank God we recorded this interview because Dr. Andersen didn't stop throwing out pearls of practical experience that helped him integrate humor into the culture of his college. We asked him the dumb questions like, "What quotes do you live by?" Without hesitation he rattled off Victor Borge's famous line, "The laugh is the shortest distance between two people." It is one thing to say it, but it is another thing to use it to move your organization ahead. He believed that if a businessperson was to use humor, you had to show them the bottom line results—and there are plenty of benefits to show.

Dr. Andersen had his own struggles as president of another college trying to convince the school to adopt a fun and playful humor attitude. Criticisms abounded, even in the community in accepting a college president as a local humor columnist. The old guard didn't believe a college president should involve himself in such trivial behavior. But forge on he did!

Dr. Andersen said:

Let me give you just one example that occurred during a difficult negotiation process. It is a real example of a large firm that I won't mention that's very close to the school. In 1991, I taught a graduate course entitled 'Creative and Intuitive Aspects of Management' to 25 managers and executives. We explored the power of humor to create a more relaxed, informal, and imaginative climate for conducting everyday business as well as for addressing crises which periodically confront every organization.

In my lecture I stress that humor enhances intuition and creativity by removing the barriers of apprehension, fear, and anxiety that inevitably accompany high stress situations. I challenged my students in the course to find a way to infiltrate humor into an important activity or event in the coming week, whether at work or at home. Perhaps some of you are preparing to face a major problem or challenge which could be tackled in a different, more effective way with a dose of humor. I did not expect most of my students to take me up on my offer. Nevertheless I asked for reports the following week. Three hands went up, including a volunteer I never suspected would have experimented with something quite this unusual. I called on him first. He was a middle-aged executive who had worked for one of the largest regional employers for more than twenty years. Visibly nervous, he stood up and paused before speaking.

He began, *'The contract with our employee union expires in three months. As most of you probably know from reading the newspapers for the past couple of years, we haven't had the greatest of labor relations at our company. Our last two sets of negotiations got off to a rocky start and quickly led to impasse.'* Almost all heads in the room nodded. Everyone seemed to be aware of the labor problems associated with this large firm, especially when a new contract was being negotiated.

The volunteer continued. *'During the past month it seemed that both sides were preparing to go down the same road again. The usual posturing during negotiations was happening. All of the accusations, charges, countercharges, bickering, and lobbying. We felt that the tone set at the initial session was essential to the overall series of meetings which would follow, but in the past, as soon as the representatives from both sides entered the room you could cut the tension with a knife. It all went downhill after that. Defensive barriers were erected and the opportunity for meaningful dialogue was lost.'* He paused and looked directly at me. *'When Dr. Andersen suggested using humor to address a major organizational issue, my initial reaction was that he was from a different planet. That the real world was not an appropriate place for something perceived as frivolous and unbusinesslike. Then, driving home Monday after our class, I asked myself what I had to lose. How could things be any worse that what had occurred in the past? Our initial negotiation session was set for last Friday morning. I met with our three negotiators Wednesday afternoon. I proposed something quite radical. Their initial reaction was the same one I had when Dr. Andersen presented the challenge to our class. They thought I had been transported to another dimension.'* The class laughed. *'After we discussed the new approach at length they agreed to give it a try.'*

'First, I moved the location of the session from a large, stuffy conference facility in which a long table separated the two sides to a small employee lounge which had only easy chairs. Then, after the four negotiators from the union arrived, our three negotiators made a dramatic entrance wearing huge buttons that said, "Save time, see it our way." The four members of the union

broke up when they saw the buttons. The seven of us shared a great laugh.' He grinned reflectively. 'That never happened before. In fact I can't even recall a smile ever being exchanged. Our three negotiators then took off their buttons and handed them to their four union counterparts. We'd brought an extra one. They immediately put them on and we began the session. The atmosphere was changed and the meeting ended with positive progress. The story of the buttons made it through the company grapevine within hours. Somehow everyone knew that this time, things would be different!'

Six weeks later the volunteer informed the class that a new agreement had been approved by both sides. I cannot recall a more rewarding moment I've ever had as a teacher. Could it have backfired? Probably, but again, you might have the reaction sometimes, what could you possibly lose? Okay, but you'd have to know the person who was there in the class, because changing the mindset is difficult to do sometimes.

Dr. Andersen explained the struggles he went through trying to receive acceptance of his fun and playful behavior in an educational environment. However, his greatest naysayers become believers when they see the results of his efforts.

Humor has helped to gain national recognition for this small community college—something a more conservative posture would not have been able to do. It is our job as writers, as it is Dr. Andersen's job as a college president, to help raise the awareness of the management philosophy that utilizes humor—the *Laugh & Get Rich* philosophy—as a viable tool to productivity.

RECAP:

- It is difficult to change a mindset...but not impossible.
- A humor policy can be adopted anywhere.
- The worst of times is fertile for humor.
- If different sells, then humor is different.
- An idea and four buttons were able to change a company completely.
- The use of humor is a tension-controlling mechanism.

Ideas this gives you for your business:

_____

_____

_____

_____

_____

_____

_____

_____

_____

_____

CHAPTER 37

The Chairman of the Bored

Dave Fitzgerald, professional speaker/comedian

"Comedians are just people who found a way to complain and get paid for it!"

– Dave Fitzgerald

Our friend Dave Fitzgerald calls himself a "Motivedian." He defines "Motivedian" as "a person who will laugh you into action." Sounds like fun. Dave puts his money where his fun is. While serving on the board of directors for the New England Speakers Association, he brought his own twist to many of his duties.

Here is an example of a problem he battled with humor. Dave was handling the directory for the year, a monstrous task that no one else wanted in this volunteer association. We all have deadlines that we feel are not as deadly as others, so human nature gets us to procrastinate. When the deadline comes due, since our friends are handling the task, we feel that our excuses will not be questioned. We feel we can get away with more.

How do you communicate an urgent message when excuses, historically, are not policed? Dave's answer: Humunicate! Communicate with humor! The Cannoli Principle in action! A message is more digestible when you use humor. This is the letter Dave sent out to the NESA members:

Hello Fellow NESA Members,

This is an important message!

Due to an inordinate amount of calamities that have hit our members during the same week that our directory stuff is due, we have been forced to extend our DROP DEAD DEADLINE for Directory Ads and listing info to October 31st!

You may want to contact your friends to be sure they are OK!

Here are the responses:

My dog ate it! (4) or My dog &*%$ on it! (3)
Staff person ate it! (3) or Staff person &*%$ on it! (1)
Staff person ran off with my checkbook! (1)
Staff person ran off with my spouse! (1)
My child turned it in for homework! (1)
It disintegrated in the washing machine! (1)
My printer messed up! (7)

I am happy to report that there was not one instance where the NESA member was at fault!

This is good news for anyone who wanted to run an ad and thought they were out of time! YOU CAN DO IT!

Everyone please get your stuff together and get it in!!

Did you see the subtle messages in the letter? Do you think this letter got read? Do you think it would have been as effective without the humor? Do you see how the humor says "It's okay. You are not alone, but please get your material in," without getting angry or allowing the reader to get defensive? Dave is truly a *motivedian* and uses humor very effectively.

RECAP:

- Motivedian: someone who can laugh you into action. Do you have any in your organization? Are they being fully utilized?

- This is a real-life example. How can you use this idea to help you?

- Dave uses the common theme that human nature causes us to blame others. What common theme are you up against with your problem or audience?

Ideas this gives you for your business:

CHAPTER 38

H-U-M-O-R...
That's How I
Spell Relief

Sherwin Greenblatt,
COO Bose® Corporation

"Humor is the greatest tension reliever."

– Sherwin Greenblatt

D arren and Rick's very first interview was with Sherwin Greenblatt, the Chief Operating Officer of Bose® Corporation, a leading innovator in sound reproduction technology and the world's largest manufacturer of loud speakers and music systems for homes, automobiles, and public places. Most have heard of its critically acclaimed music systems. You've heard the old adage, "Been around since Day 1." Greenblatt literally has been. He was the first employee hired by Dr. Amar Bose when the company was founded.

Though a company must have excellent products and services to survive, it is how its leaders think that determines its success and longevity. Darren and Rick knew when they walked into Greenblatt's office that they were in the right place. In the corner of his office stands a coatrack wearing a traditional Santa Claus hat and a fireman's hat. Everything else in the office looks like any other executive's office. That is what humor is, the normal, just off-center.

The executives we interviewed were very professional and believe in the power of humor as a tool for business and life. They do not wear red noses and clown shoes to intentionally motivate people. They allow fun to be a part of the way they do business, for the sake of sanity and better business.

Greenblatt remembers the days when he knew every employee by name. That is no longer possible. What he does these days is make a presentation to new employees during their orientation. Darren sat in on a presentation and says that Greenblatt is a wonderful speaker, both poignant and fun. He makes light of the humble beginnings of the company, which creates a sense of pride in the employees. He humanizes a huge company for the newly hired. Simple and powerful. It comes through that he not only enjoys it, but that the company cares about its employees. He is very approachable, even having lunch each day in the cafeteria.

Why did Rick and Darren interview Sherwin Greenblatt? Because of a quote that an employee told Darren about which some employees hang in their offices to ward off the Funsuckers. This quote sums up the *Laugh & Get Rich* philosophy and the people who use this way of conducting business:

> *There is no reason why you can't relax, laugh, and do the things that one considers play while you are working. I think that's the healthiest and best mixture. We certainly have enough stress that we can use some fun and play.*

Who said it? Sherwin Greenblatt.
Think about it and from whom it comes.

Really think...

How would some executives in your company react to this idea? We are doing this to emphasize the importance of this way of thinking. You read books to get ideas, suggestions, and information to add to your own personal philosophy. And for those readers who are in a hurry to finish the book, we want you to have a feeling of accomplishment as you reflect and turn the pages.

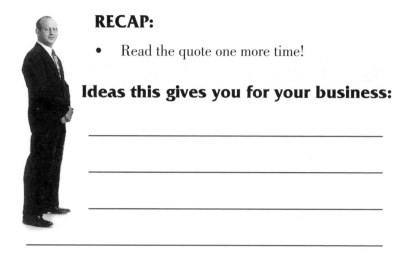

RECAP:

- Read the quote one more time!

Ideas this gives you for your business:

_____

_____

_____

_____

_____

_____

_____

_____

_____

_____

_____

_____

_____

_____

_____

CHAPTER 39

Interview in the Fridge

Bob Wendover,
Leadership Resources, Inc.

"We spend six months to six years choosing a spouse with whom we spend two hours a day, and we spend anywhere from a half hour to an hour choosing someone with whom we spend eight to ten hours a day. What is wrong with this picture?"

– Bob Wendover

B
ob Wendover is a human resource consultant and the author of four books. His works include *Smart Hiring for Your Business*, *High Performance Hiring*, and *Two-Minute Motivation: How to Hire Superior Performance*. This is impressive, but why did we interview him?

Bob believes highly in the use of humor, especially in his department. He likes to have fun at work himself. An employee named Tracy, who had been working with Bob for a while, was a very young and very good worker. She went out one weekend and decided to get her nose pierced—at a time when this was not widely accepted. When she came in on Monday morning she went to see Bob like a sad puppy who knew it had done wrong. Before she revealed her new jewelry she asked him, "Promise me you won't get upset?" After he got past his initial shock, and sensing her "state," he thought to himself, how can we have a little fun with this? (Sounds like one of the three powerful questions doesn't it? Are you finding a pattern here?)

He could sense the tension in her. So he said that if he were to take her with him to an appointment, the two of them might have to discuss this new development, but because her work involved contact by phone, "it does not make a difference to me, unless of course, the thing whistles when you talk." This brought them both to laughter, allowing them to talk further without the obvious tension in the air.

When hiring, Bob tries to get a reading on a candidate's ability to work with others. He believes that we need to find out as much as we can in a fairly short period of time about that person's personality because we have to practically live with that person. Not to mention the fact that we are going to pay them a lot of money and our livelihood is going to be dependent upon their performance. Bob believes he can teach anyone how to do the average thing, but if she or he cannot do it with a sense of humor and a personality that inspires others around them, the candidate may not be who he is looking for.

From his research, Bob told us that Holiday Inn actually takes the time and effort to count the number of times an applicant smiles during an interview. He said their philosophy follows the belief that it is easier to take someone and teach them the processes than it is to teach them to smile.

More of his studies led him to discover what happens at Southwest Airlines. They perform group interviews and ask all applicants to get up and talk about themselves for two minutes in front of the group. The interviewers take careful note of how the audience responds to the person's speaking, and less so to what the applicant says. This also allows them to watch the applicants in the audience to see if they are paying attention, an indication of team players and a deeper picture of their true attitudes.

The Interview Process:

There is a plethora of books on the market about how to get hired and how to respond to interview questions. All of which is great for the applicant—but this makes it tougher on the human resource professional to discover the "true" person during the interview process and whether they are right for the job. Most questions of a predictable nature can be responded to in a prepared manner by the candidate. In a sense, what the candidate does is to perform for the interviewer. So the sum of information learned by the interviewer carries less weight in the hiring-decision process.

Bob recommends:

#1 - No Static Cling

Get applicants out of the interview room and walk them around. It is difficult for people to walk in an unfamiliar environment and not concentrate partially on the walking. If people are thrown off guard, they are less able to effectively replicate a prepared answer. This does not mean they cannot answer; it means the response tends to be more truthful and genuine. Bob feels that when he is walking candidates through an unfamiliar environment with strangers around them, they are more likely to get into a conversation. Bob even tells humorous stories about workplace events to intentionally loosen them up. Often, he says, applicants will respond with stories of their own.

#2 - Just Step Into My Fridge

Bob brings applicants into the environment in which they will be working. If you want to hire a frozen food merchandiser, interview them in the walk-in refrigerator. There are warm-blooded people and cold-blooded people. If an applicant starts shivering after a few minutes, this is probably not the person for this particular position. Though such a job may be an extreme case, it makes the principle easy to remember. You can work subtle variations for your applicants. You are looking for their innate comfort in the environments in which they will be working.

While much depends on the position for which the applicant is applying, Bob feels strongly that a "sense of humor" is a must for people who have direct contact with others, both internally and externally. For managers and supervisory personnel, he believes that is part of what is required.

#3 - Don't Look for Stars, Look for Patterns

Observe more! Look for the patterns in how people think and act. Bob tells a story about Penny, his receptionist, who had to answer several different phone lines. One of the phone numbers was one key away from the phone number of an evangelical ministry that sells audio tapes. One afternoon Penny got a call.

Penny: Customer service, how can I help you?

Caller: Yea, I wanna buy a tape on stress reduction.

Penny: I think you dialed the wrong number. What number are you dialing?

Caller: The ministry.

Penny: I am sorry, that number is 7-400 and you dialed 7-700.

Caller: (Pause) But this is customer service?

Penny: Well yes, but not the right customer service.

Caller: Well, how can you be customer service if you are not willing to help me?

Penny: I am trying to help you, but I can't.

Caller: (Big huff and a sigh of disgust) I am trying to call to get a tape on stress reduction, and if you are not going to help me, I am going to hang up!

Penny: Praise the Lord! (and she hung up the phone).

Think about what this 20-second conversation illustrates. You can pick up all kinds of qualities about a person if you are carefully observing. Did you notice Penny's ability to think quickly? How about her communication style? Although employees readily share on-the-job anecdotes like this one, job applicants need prompting. If you can get 10 stories out of an applicant, you begin to see their patterns. This is what will help you to truly see how they act and think.

#4 - It's Story Time

Have applicants tell you stories! Period! Bob's interview style is not "Can you do this?" Rather it is, "Tell me a story about how you would approach this." He also asks for stories about the stuff that is funny that happens on the job.

Bob's Bottom-Line Beliefs:

- Here they are in a nutshell. (Why is "nutshell" so widely used? Would a thimble be considered a smaller, more impressive unit? That's another book…)

- Having fun with applicants helps get them past their nervousness and shows the real person.

- Humor demonstrates a person's level of self-esteem.

- Humor demonstrates a person's level of competence in building rapport.

- The higher you go in an organization, the less valued are technical skills and the more valued are rapport skills.

- Hire for humor, by humor, with humor!

RECAP:

- We spend 6 months to 6 years choosing a spouse with whom we spend two hours a day, and we spend anywhere from a half hour to an hour choosing someone with whom we spend 8 to 10 hours a day. What is wrong with this picture?

- Holiday Inn actually takes the time and effort to count the number of times an applicant smiles during an interview.

- Having fun with applicants helps to get past the nervousness and see the real person.

- Hire for humor, by humor, with humor!

Ideas this gives you for your business:

_____

_____

_____

_____

_____

_____

_____

_____

_____

CHAPTER 40

Inside the Mind of an Entertainment Shopping King

Barry Tatelman, Co-Owner, Jordan's Furniture

"People don't want to go to a furniture store, they want to be entertained."

– Barry Tatelman, Jordan's Furniture

W hy do Darren and Rick consider Barry Tatelman the "Entertainment Shopping King?" Quite simply, he is. We have touched on this company in a previous chapter, but Darren and Rick felt it would be incredibly valuable to talk to him and find out about his business philosophy. When Darren does his keynote presentations on profiting from humor, he always asks the audiences in New England, "By a show of hands how many of you know who Barry and Eliot are?" More than half the members of the audience, without any more prompting, raise their hands. When Darren says, "The guys from Jordan's Furniture," another 25 percent go up. Significantly, the hands go up accompanied by smiles. This is the Clown Concept in action again. Barry and Eliot use many of the principles in this book. What Darren and Rick have done is focused the subject, made the concepts universal, and put a name to them.

Many reading this book may say, "It's nice that all these people know Barry and Eliot and smile, but what are the numbers?" Well, for those of you who need numbers for credibility, let us educate you about Jordan's Furniture with some numbers, facts, and fun ideas.

- Jordan's Furniture has grown from 15 employees to more than 1,000 employees in 25 years.

- As Jordan's Furniture continues to grow, sales per square foot also increase. Jordan's averages sales of $900 per square foot, whereas most furniture retailers average sales of $150 per square foot.

- An average store turns over inventory one to two times a year. Jordan's turns over its inventory 13 times a year.

- Although most retailers spend approximately 7 percent of their income for marketing and advertising, Jordan's Furniture spends about 2 percent.

- Jordan's is planning on doubling its size in the next few years (they are currently the largest furniture store in New England).

- Jordan's was chosen **Retailer of the Year in the U.S.** by the National Home Furnishings Association (out of 12,000 retailers).

- Jordan's was named **Guerrilla Marketer of the Year** ("Guerrilla Marketing Handbook" by Jay Levenson and Seth Godin).

- Barry and Eliot were chosen **Men of the Year** by the Tri-state Home Furnishings Association.

- Jordan's received **Telly Awards** for many of its advertising campaigns.

- It was named **Retailer of the Year** by GERS Retail Systems.

- *"The most unusual furniture store in the world"* said *Home Furnishings Daily* and *Furniture Today*

- Another honor: **Entrepreneur of the Year/Social Responsibility** (Ernst & Young).

- In the field of education, Jordan's created and funded a media literacy program to teach 5th graders the critical thinking skills needed to understand the growing role of the media. Approximately 100 students per day participate in this program.

- Jordan's invested $2.5 million in its MOM (Motion Odyssey Movie Ride). More than $300,000 has been donated to non-profit organizations from the proceeds of the ride.

- **Furniture Bank**—Approximately 60 pieces of product a week are donated to the Massachusetts Coalition for the Homeless's Furniture Bank.

- **Streetcar Named Dessert**—Monthly proceeds from the streetcar, located inside their Natick, Massachusetts, store goes to MetroWest charities.

- **Fundraisers on Bourbon Street**—Non-profit organizations are given the opportunity to hold their fundraisers or company events on Bourbon Street in the Natick, Massachusetts, store on designated Sunday evenings.

- **Holiday Gifts for "Head Start" Children**—Each year, the employees of Jordan's Furniture purchase gifts for the students in local Head Start programs.

The company is also known for its **JORDANisms**; Barry and Eliot love to rename furniture items and put their own twist on things, such as:

- **Underprices**—These are not "sales" or promotion-driven price cuts. The store has low prices all the time. (Note: Huge lesson here! Darren and Rick believe that to stand out and get ahead you have to be a contrarian in your industry. Retailers tend to think you have to have bigger "sales" to compete. Barry and Eliot have crushed this myth! How is everyone else doing it in your industry and how can you be better?)

- **J-Team**—All Jordan's employees. They are all trained to make "raving fans" out of customers.

- **Marshmallow**—a sofa.

- **Fabricadabra**—a computer program that allows customers to see their fabric selections.

- **Oops Proof**—fabric protection.

- **Sofas with a Secret**—motion furniture.

- **Fact Tag**—each piece of furniture is tagged with one that tells the manufacturer, the warranty, the size, special care instructions, components, and so on. Manufacturers are required to "sign off" on this information because honesty is the only way to do business at Jordan's.

WHERE DID IT ALL START?

When Darren interviewed Barry he found him very open, sincere, and straightforward. Darren found this delightful! When asked about the origin of Jordan's way of doing business, Barry was insistent about the importance of a good foundation. The company was started in 1918 by Barry and Eliot's grandfather, Samuel. He sold furniture out of the back of a truck until 1926 when he opened the first store in Waltham, Massachusetts. In the late 1930s their father, Edward, joined the business.

Barry said that he and his brother, Eliot, inherited a good, honest business from their grandfather. Building from that foundation was the key to growth and survival. In the 1950s and 1960s, the brothers helped out on weekends and summers. Eliot got paid 10 cents an hour to dust and Barry got 5 cents. (Barry saids that Eliot was overpaid!) In 1973 the brothers took over the business. They stopped advertising on the back page of the Waltham paper and started on radio.

As most business owners know, running a business is much more than a 40-hour-a-week job. Barry and Eliot figured that if they were going to have to work 70 to 90 hours a week, the least they could do was to make it fun! Barry said that their way of doing business evolved slowly from this concept.

OPENING UP THE CUSTOMER

Any basic sales course will tell you that one of the first steps to making a sale is getting a customer's attention. If you knew nothing about the store, when you drove up to some of the Jordan's stores you would immediately know there is something different about them. They have pink parking lot lines! Subtle, but it gets your attention. It changes customer expectations. Immediately, people start thinking, "This is going to be different." Then they start looking for more subtleties around them. Being more aware, customers are more "in the moment" than if they walked into the store with blinders on.

Breaking the train of thought with customers is not easy. Everyone has so much going on in their hectic lives that it can be difficult to become completely relaxed and enjoy the shopping experience. In the Jordan's store in Nashua, New Hampshire, even the olfactory sense is tickled. When you walk in the door, the aroma of freshly baked cookies delights your nose. Talk about making you feel right at home! Whatever was weighing on your mind immediately becomes lighter. This helps make customers feel better, so it opens them up. People like to feel better!

What else does Jordan's do out of the ordinary? In their Avon, Massachusetts, store they feature robotronics, animatronics, smells throughout the showroom, balloons on weekends, umbrella service, and hot dogs at the customer pickup location. The Avon store also houses the 48-seat, four-story movie screen for their Motion Odyssey Movie (MOM) ride. The Natick store presents a Bourbon Street in New Orleans theme, complete with full-sized building facades, a riverboat, robotics, and live music. Mardi Gras happens every hour on Bourbon Street with a 9-minute, multi-media show, including celebrity robotics, a music video, and a 40-foot jester. The Natick store also has a full-service restaurant right inside! As you can imagine, these are not your average furniture showrooms.

BARRY'S BELIEFS

When we interview top executives about humor and its use in business, a strange and recurring theme arises. These executives are all extremely passionate about the use of humor. Levity is never taken lightly. In fact there seems to be no subject more serious to them than their belief in the power of humor! Barry seemed to be the epitome of this statement. There is a sign in Jordan's Furniture that highlights this philosophy. Every executive in the country should think about it and relate it to their business. The sign says:

There is no business that's not show business.

What better way to stand out in any industry than to be the leader and become known as the "most fun"? It goes back to Michelle's Rule: We do business with people we have fun with. It starts with something as simple as letterhead. Why do some companies have full-color letterhead and others black and white? It's about image. Image is "show business." Every business has an image, like it or not. Thus, every business is in show business. Whether it is a Broadway show or a school play is up to you. Every aspect with a connection to the outside world is a separate stage. Manage that stage wisely. People are judging you on that show whether you manage it or not.

What is the basis for the processes and the creativity that Barry and his brother exercise? Belief. Every action we take is based on some belief that we have. Some of the key beliefs that direct some of Barry's actions are: "Humor gets more out of people"; "If people are happy they are more efficient"; and the old adage, "You get more with sugar than with vinegar."

The benefits from these beliefs are obvious. According to Barry, if you want employees to be more efficient, "the process" itself may not be the only thing on which to focus. It may be that making the employees happy will make everything flow more smoothly, more quickly.

Darren asked Barry where he feels humor makes the most impact on the bottom line. Barry replied, "Humor relaxes customers, and it gains their trust and their business." Though Jordan's believes in baking cookies in their stores, they are adamant about not being cookie-cutters. Each store is different. Though the success of MOM was great in Avon, when they built Natick they did not try the same thing. An added bonus in that difference is that if you have had a "Jordan's experience" in one store and you find yourself near another store, you might pop in just to see the difference. Not bad for a furniture store! The exact opposite of the "franchise factor." Without the initial experience being extraordinary, you probably would not have any further interest. Though their Natick store boasts 120,000 square feet, they have even bigger plans for a future store, and they guarantee it won't be anything like any of the others. This is the epitome of the old line, "What will those guys think of next?"

Because we have written about how humor can be used in an interview process, Darren was really looking forward to Barry's perspective on hiring. Darren loves it when an unexpected answer to a question comes out in an interview. It means that we learn something new and fascinating. When he asked Barry about how they find "fun" people, Darren was shocked by Barry's saying they do not! They look for *good* people. Barry said that the fun happens through assimilation. Employees see others around them having fun so they have a natural tendency to want to have fun, too. As in any environment, people tend to assimilate their surroundings. Jordan's does not try to hire "funny" people. Jordan's already created an environment in which fun is welcomed, and though new hires may not be used to that with previous employers, fun becomes simply a natural occurrence.

How do Barry and Eliot determine what new ideas they will implement? Barry explained, "If it sounds fun, is unique, and makes sense, we try it." It is a simple and powerful business philosophy. Have they ever made a mistake? They usually put themselves in the shoes of both the customer and employee. They think through from the beginning to the end thoroughly. Only one time did they not successfully anticipate the customer's view. They once had the J-Team customer service warehouse employees dress in tuxedos to wash customer car windows. As the customers came around to pick up their purchases, the team would run and "do windows." Customers were a little shocked, as enthusiastic people came running at their cars. It was unexpected, and not entirely welcomed. Barry said that it was the one time they did not completely factor in the viewpoint of the customer. He said the window washing was a good idea—it was just not executed perfectly.

If JFK had done a seminar on leadership and success, Darren and Rick think he would have wrapped it up in a proclamation, "Ask not what your employees can do for your company, ask what your company can do for your employees!" Want to create goodwill and loyalty with your employees? Think about that statement. Unfortunately, once something is done for employees repeatedly, it becomes expected and not appreciated—until they talk to someone who works elsewhere and who does not have the same luxuries.

What have you done for your employees that is fun, different, and enjoyed by all? The latest from Barry and Eliot was to close their stores for a day, charter four passenger planes, and bring all 1,400 employees to Bermuda for the day! Do you think they have to place many help wanted ads?

"Humor in the workplace" is a *nice* concept, but what business people want to know is how and why. The *Laugh & Get Rich* philosophy goes beyond "fun in the workplace." It is looking at work as a fun place. So many people talk about humor in the workplace. The Jordan's Furniture guys don't talk about it, they just plain "do it." We are glad we could get Barry to stop doing it long enough to talk about it.

RECAP:

- **"YOU CAN ENJOY YOUR LIFE & STILL COME IN FIRST!"** – Barry

- Jordan's does not try to hire funny people. They hire good people, create an environment of fun, and encourage humor. The fun comes from assimilation.

- Humor gets more out of people.

- The "core" of business is knowing "people."

- Employees must "buy in" to the concept to make the fun work for you.

- "If people are happy they are more efficient."

- "Humor relaxes customers... gains their trust and their business."

Ideas this gives you for your business:

_____

_____

_____

_____

_____

_____

_____

_____

CHAPTER 41

Humor vs. Goliath

Paul Stone,
Baldwin & Stone Advertising Agency

---

*"My job is not to sell the customer,
but to create a sense of affection—
a positive attitude toward my client."*

– Paul Stone

H uge successes do not come without enormous challenges. Most of us know the story of David and Goliath, the great underdog story. Everyone loves the underdog. Unless, of course, you are the underdog faced with a huge business challenge.

WB Mason was a $10 million (in 1986 dollars) office furniture and supply company with its headquarters in Brockton, Massachusetts. Located 22 miles outside of Boston, no one in the big city had ever heard of them. This would not necessarily be a problem, except that they wanted to grow into the Boston market, which already had national chains with a strong hold.

Darren was cast in a commercial for WB Mason and that is where he met Paul Stone, principal of Baldwin and Stone, Inc., a Boston-based advertising firm. In talking to Paul, Darren realized that the WB Mason story was the essence of the *Laugh & Get Rich* philosophy.

The goal of the new ad campaign was to successfully enter the Boston market. One problem was public opinion; namely, the sentiment *who cares?* WB Mason was trying to become a small fish in a big pond. To come in and make outlandish statements when no one has heard of you can come off as arrogant, if not done properly.

But it's okay to make outlandish statements if it is done with humor. If the humor is not cruel it can open customers up to the pitch. This is the Cannoli Principle in action: the message is more digestible when wrapped in humor. Paul's challenge was to "not try" and to "not do too much." He did not try to make the sale, which is often the mistake in a campaign that attempts to accomplish too much. He tried to just have fun, to create an image of enjoyment, and to let people know what WB Mason did, while staying consistent with the image he had already created outside of Boston.

It was also extremely helpful that WB Mason was not afraid to spend the dollars necessary to accomplish such a task. This was another key to the success of the campaign. Many people try to run an ad on a limited budget and expect that customers are going to just flock to their doors. There is a reason why most TV ads run for a minimum of 13 weeks. Rome wasn't built in a day and neither was any successful advertising campaign.

With the help of Baldwin and Stone they wanted to create an image for the company that would make them seem different, strong, and lasting. They also wanted to show the public that they did not take themselves too seriously. This image needed to be for the total company, not just the ads on television.

When Paul was brought into the company, WB Mason had not really done any advertising campaigns in Boston, although they had been clients of Baldwin and Stone for 10 years. Together, they chose to build an image around old-time values. They wanted to associate good, warm feelings about their products. This would not be easily or quickly achieved. So they developed a character who personified the real WB Mason. They painted their delivery trucks to look like 1898 circus trucks (WB Mason was founded in 1898). The TV ads appeared to be filmed in scratchy black and white and as if they'd come from the 1940s. They had the attitude of "let's have fun!" This was a company willing to do anything to get and keep a customer. When they started the ad campaign in Boston, the ads had a sense of the "Normandy Invasion," showing war planes flying to the rescue. The company slogan was, "Who but WB Mason." The point, again, was to have fun and poke fun at themselves (no one gets offended that way), allowing people to identify with them. The Boston Invasion campaign was to be a personable and likeable image. It was not, "Hey, buy from us, we got great prices!"

What else was essential to the success of the campaign? Paul Stone said that director Bob Nole was able to keep the affectionate tone running throughout the commercials. The campaign has allowed the tone to be remembered, which helps condition the audience and differentiates the advertising. Paul told Darren of an observation he'd made one day while watching Bob Hope. Though he was enjoying Bob Hope, he realized that the comedian was not funny anymore. Nonetheless, as Paul watched he had a smile on his face. He had been conditioned over time to enjoying Mr. Hope's earlier humor. All of us have experienced this effect in one form or another, giving a little extra grease to people we like based on the enjoyment they gave us in the past. We can even find ourselves defending them to naysayers.

Baldwin and Stone are firm believers in working with serendipity, never against it. When the campaign was being launched in Boston, it was kicked off with a high exposure Super Bowl commercial. The tag line for this commercial was originally written for a man to say, "Who are these guys?" When they got to the point of auditioning for the role, a 7-year-old actress was brought in to read. The line she read was, "Daddy, who are these people?" But when the actress took her mark and delivered the line, it came out as, "Who are those wonderful people?" She was so charming that the scripted line was changed. Paul and his team thought this would charm the audience as well. He had no idea how successful his intuition would be.

It takes confidence to be open to new ideas when undertaking such big endeavors. People who are always on the lookout for what's best and do not allow their egos to get in the way of their goals usually find serendipity on their side. This serendipitous line has now become part of all the WB Mason Commercials. Thirteen years later, WB Mason is still growing and still sticking to its image. What are people in Boston saying? "WB Mason trucks are everywhere!" Not quite, but the trucks do stand out and are remembered, giving the impression of being everywhere. People even joke with the delivery people! When customers say to them, "Who are these wonderful people?" it's an example of the inclusionary humor we talk about. Another powerful image creation is having customers themselves become part of the campaign, joking with the WB Mason sales force.

What do people say when they see a salesperson coming from your company? You can't buy that kind of advertising. Well, yes, you can. WB Mason did, but it took time, money, and some creative people. When "who are those wonderful people?" is repeated with a certain amount of energy and interest to a salesperson, that is a sign of a strong relationship. This relationship also allows mistakes to be made without a loyal customer's jumping ship to the competition. It gives the company leeway— as long as the company corrects its mistakes and takes care of the customer in the end.

Paul stressed that a business cannot survive on humor alone. What it can do is to greatly enhance an already strong company that has powerful customer service. We have heard this from many of the executives we interviewed. Our guess is the executives we interviewed who never mentioned it, assumed it all the way.

"Nothing kills a bad company better than good advertising," Paul said. Most interviewees have said that humor and fun were an integral part of their growth. But only as a backing to a strong company with powerful customer service. Darren asked Paul how important humor was to the campaign and growth of WB Mason. Paul stated that it was impossible to put a number or percentage on it. He said it was definitely an integral part of the growth and could not be separated from the whole.

What are the numbers? Thirteen years later, WB Mason has grown to a $175 million company. For those of you without a calculator handy, that is 17 times its size in just 13 years. It's tough to argue with that kind of success. "Who but WB Mason!" Or as we like to say, "Who but humor!"

RECAP:

- Business cannot live on humor alone.

- Take your best weapons, put them in the slingshot of humor, and Goliath will fall. You've gotta have good weapons already.

- "My job is not to sell the customer, but to create a sense of affection and positive attitude toward my client, WB Mason." —Paul Stone. Don't try to do too much with an ad campaign.

- Remember the tone.

- Leggo my ego! Don't let egos get in the way of goals.

- Work with serendipity, never against.

- The bottom line is the bottom line.

- Who but humor!

Ideas this gives you for your business:

_____

_____

_____

_____

_____

_____

_____

_____

CHAPTER 42

MOCHa HAGoTDI

Daniel Wolf, President Cape Air

*"We are liberating employees to do
what human beings like to do,
have fun and be creative."*

– Daniel Wolf, Cape Air

Two questions come to mind. Who is Cape Air? What is MOCHa HAGoTDI? Cape Air is the largest, non-affiliated regional airline in the United States. Its headquarters are located on Cape Cod in Massachusetts. It services more than 400,000 passengers per year and is growing. MOCHa HAGoTDI is not the newest flavor of gourmet coffee; it is a way of doing business, it is a philosophy, it is the essence of this book. Daniel Wolf, president of the company, and his management staff developed this acronym. The acronym stands for **M**ake **O**ur **C**ustomers **H**appy—**H**ave **A** **Go**od **T**ime **D**oing **I**t. It is simple, crisp, and powerful. Most important, the philosophy enables Cape Air to be stronger and more profitable.

Dan and his staff have created this philosophy as a breeding ground for spontaneity, creativity, and resourcefulness. It creates an atmosphere in which these basic human desires are encouraged to flow. It is a safe atmosphere in which to take a risk. This is one employer Thomas Edison probably could have worked for.

Could your work environment be categorized in this way? How is risk viewed at your company? What will they think of next? This breeding ground has already had its successes. As a company, Cape Air wanted to bring art and culture to the community. They wanted to do so in a creative way. Being located near an art community they decided to start there. They wanted to find an artist and give him or her a different kind of canvas. The artist they chose is known as Jurek. They gave him a plane and free license. The program is called "Art in Flight." The result of 160 hours of painstaking work was a most spectacular original work of art. His masterpiece depicts the destination of the plane. An aircraft that serves Key West has its nose as a realistic shark's head, a parrot's head, a likeness of Tony Tarracino (former mayor of Key West), and the face of a weatherbeaten pirate. The plane's wings have turtles scurrying all over them. This art with its eye-catching colors literally covers the plane. It is sure to cause double takes when first spotted. This idea did not come from the marketing department, but it ended up bringing great marketing benefits such as differentiation and PR. The important point is that creative ideas blossom in a fun environment.

Through MOCHa HAGoTDI, the airline developed the RAT award: **R**ecognized **A**nd **T**hanked. It is a trophy with a rat on it. Why a rat? So people are not motivated for the prize or for the recognition. Cape Air just wants its people to be creative and have fun. Cape Air also developed contests like "As the Fog Rises" and established a Fun Committee. It even considered taking its reservations over the phone using duck voices. How many of you have Fun Committees? How many committees have you been on that have been fun? Why? Why not?

We asked Dan how his MOCHA HAGoTDI philosophy had an impact on the bottom line. Dan mentioned three ways. First, Dan believes strongly that his company's way of doing business creates the bottom line. More passengers come back to them more frequently because of the way they do business. When Dan described this bottom line result it was as if he was reading Chapter 18 about Michelle's Rule right out of this book. Except that Dan never read the manuscript to this book. Cape Air lives it. Rick and Darren did not make up the concept. It was like gravity—it was always there. We just put a label on it.

It is important to clarify that we are not talking about professional comedians working for Cape Air. These are simply *real* people doing *real* work who just happen to like to have fun. You do not walk up to a Cape Air ticket counter and be rolling in the aisles laughing as you board the plane. If you "experience" these people you'll notice a difference, even though you might not put your finger on it right away.

What you find at a ticket counter are employees with a license to MOCHa HAGoTDI. For example, at one counter the usual procedure is to hand out red and yellow boarding cards. When the time comes to board you hear a call for yellow boarding cards. One employee came up with the idea of substituting fruit for boarding cards. That's right, employees handed out apples, oranges, and bananas. When the time was right you heard over the intercom, "Will all of the *bananas* please proceed to gate 5." That humor is more powerful than a good joke and longer-lasting.

We tend to forget jokes, but the image of being handed a banana instead of a boarding card brings a smile and a positive memory that lasts. Just as with Mac the pig, passengers also have an ice breaker in common with everyone else on the flight and with the employees. That builds loyalty. The idea did not come from Dan, but no one probably enjoyed hearing it more than he did. MOCHa in action!

The second way MOCHa HAGoTDI makes an impact on the bottom line is to build trust. This is something we had not really heard before. Trust in co-workers and trust in the company. Dan pointed out a great observation of his, that there seems to be a direct correlation between trust and humor. When we have fun and laugh with people they become our friends and we open up to them. With this happening, it is natural to trust them more. A deeper trust in co-workers and the company is the breeding ground for an employee's loyalty to the company. What does this mean to the bottom line? Dan believes that it directly reduces costs. Although this is not why the philosophy was developed, a huge benefit derives from it.

It was easy to notice an "openness" at the offices of Cape Air that we did not understand right away. It was like being among family—not perfect, not blue chip, not phony, but having a level of trust and comfort among its members. In this environment, Dan says they do not waste time "policing" employees and spending valuable resources trying to safeguard against petty loss or punching time clocks. They also trust employees to track their own vacation time. When you trust others, they trust and become loyal to you. Dan does not believe in punishing all for the deeds of few. Employees are presumed innocent and good people. That's what people want. That is what they get. That is what they give.

Cape Air also treats its customers in a similar manner. Dan says that he transports 400,000 passengers per year, and he believes in giving all customers the benefit of the doubt for the few who try to take advantage of this trust. This is building relationships; this is building a business.

The third impact on the bottom line is lower turnover. Yes, Darren and Rick know you've heard this before. Many times we have to hear things more than once before we really "get it." Lower turnover equals lower costs in training, and other obvious benefits. Let's not talk about the benefits, though; we've done that. Let's talk about the how and the why. Once the MOCHa HAGoTDI philosophy was in place, it became easier to hire employees into it, Dan explained. He said this was a *key* factor in the success of the philosophy. The company had a much clearer vision of what it was about and who would work best in this environment.

Knowing what to look for also changed the interview process. In interviews, applicants for Cape Air are not asked standard questions. They are asked questions such as, "Tell us about the last funny thing that happened to you." This is very similar to

Bob Wendover's style. We guess that funny human resource people think alike. Why? Because it works for them. It is not about hiring people in the right way—it is about hiring the right people. They need to fit into your way of doing business.

Everyone talks about turnover and the cost associated with that. How about pre-turnover productivity? This is the time when the company gets the least value out of the employee. It is also the time when the ill feelings that become lodged in the employee's brain ferment and ripen. We wonder what the "cost" is for this. It cannot be cheap, but choosing the right people from the start can minimize it.

It is important to note that most of the management people at Cape Air were already firm believers in having fun. They did not just decide that it was a stuffy place to work so one day they would develop this "fun" philosophy. The philosophy helped crystallize what they were trying to create and its purpose, so the management made it a formal way of doing business. MOCHa HAGoTDI was made clear and was rolled out like a red carpet for all to walk down if they chose to.

The new philosophy was introduced through a hilarious slide show for employees and their spouses. (In one slide Dan was wearing just diapers. Humble Humor strikes again.) The new way of doing business was embraced by most, but not all. After it became "official," a few people did leave because it was just not right for them. That is okay. That is what it is all about—having the right people all rowing in the same direction with similar beliefs. Lower turnover equals lower costs.

Herb Kelleher's Southwest Airlines has also been very successful. There is a distinct difference, however, between Southwest's way of doing business and the MOCHa HAGoTDI philosophy of Cape Air. Dan Wolf is dead set against "institutionalizing" humor. He is against repeating the same routine in different places. For example, co-workers at Cape Air who heard about the "fruit as boarding passes" idea thought it would be great to do at another ticket counter. Dan said "NO!" He wants people to come up with their own ideas and solutions, not copy someone else's. Using the fruit idea as an example, Dan is trying to avoid its getting stale. He is trying to stay away from people's saying, "Okay, it's Tuesday, who is going to get the plums?" Humor gets old, just as any process that's done in the same way again and again. People eventually grow cynical about what they are doing. This is human nature. The same routine would severely impede the ability to have an environment of spontaneity, creativity, and resourcefulness. Dan believes that "institutionalizing" stifles the individual's creativity. He also believes that a manual that tells you how to act is oppressive. A mind that is challenged is motivated. A person who is motivated is enthusiastic. Enthusiasm is contagious.

Most people believe that when they meet funny people these will be wacky clowns wearing polka dot bow ties. When most people meet Darren they do not realize he is a comedian. Many comedians are very quiet off stage and despise being asked to perform "off stage." Dan is not a comedian, either. He is an extremely professional businessman who happens to enjoy having fun.

Dan stresses that MOCHa HAGoTDI is about subtle humor. It is not a parade with trumpets blaring while the clowns step on whoopee cushions as you board the plane. It is about enjoyment and letting human beings be creative and playful. It is about a safe atmosphere to take a risk, one that nurtures spontaneity, creativity, and resourcefulness. These attributes solve a lot of problems. Who has a business that could not use people at every level who are resourceful? Is that encouraged in your environment? Where would it help most? Subtlety is not flamboyance.

Caution! One danger of creating a fun type of environment is the appropriateness of the humor. This is another key reason for choosing the right people for the job. When employees are given latitude, it is important to make sure the globe is spinning on the right axis. Humor and fun are at the other end of the spectrum from jokes. Jokes usually have a victim. Victims are always among your audience. They will be offended. Jokes can and do hurt, even when they are not intended to. It is extremely important that "appropriate" humor be defined and understood within your organization. It has got to be fun, playful, and be about "objects," not people. This cannot be emphasized enough. Mistakes have and will be made. It is much easier to avoid them on the front end.

What's next for Cape Air? On Halloween, they are going to cover the "C" in Cape Air and become Ape Air for the day. They are going to rent Ape outfits for all of the ticket people for the day. But don't look for the Apes the following year. This idea will not be "institutionalized." Dan wants to be fresh, not stale!

RECAP:

- *M*ake *O*ur *C*ustomers *Ha*ppy—*H*ave *A* *Go*od *T*ime *D*oing *I*t
- It's about subtle humor, not flamboyant humor.
- Creating an environment for spontaneity, creativity, and resourcefulness—that is empowerment!
- Creating an environment where it is safe to risk—is that powerful?
- Dan does not believe in "Institutionalizing" humor.

- The "Art in Flight" idea came from wanting to creatively spread art and culture in the community—**NOT** from the marketing department.
- How does the **MOCHa HAGoTDI** philosophy affect the bottom line?
  #1 - Customer Loyalty
  #2 - Trust
  #3 - Lower Turnover
- Define "appropriate" humor—not jokes.

Ideas this gives you for your business:

_____

_____

_____

_____

_____

CHAPTER 43

Zero to $6 Million in 6 Years – Built on a "Foundation of Fun"

Jim Laffey, CEO, Color for Real Estate

"Humor is the most underrated and overlooked value-added service you could provide... and costs you nothing."

– Jim Laffey

Stop the presses! The manuscript for this book was already sent to the editor when Darren came across the company Color for Real Estate, the largest real estate printer in the country. It specializes in printing color business cards, brochures, and postcards for real estate brokers nationwide. This company is highlighted in the "Wait Management" chapter, but Rick and Darren felt there is so much more to this company that it warrants a chapter of its own.

It will never work!

Jim Laffey and his partner, Ken Freeberg, had an idea for a company that would meet the printing needs of real estate brokers nationwide. Their difference would be making it fun. They brought this concept to the top-producing owners and brokers in the country to solicit feedback, who told Jim and Ken that in the *professional* market, "people aren't going to get it" and "people will be offended." Jim and Ken felt they had nothing to lose. Above all, they did not want to have their work be boring.

In the beginning, some people *were* offended and many did not "get it," but some *loved* it. Then, a funny thing happened. Their business started to grow. The people who loved it told their friends about the company. In Color for Real Estate's 6-year history, it has spent a total of only $900 in advertising. The rest has come from word of mouth.

Color for Real Estate started in Jim's basement. Their goal for the first year was to earn a $200 profit per day. In three years they had 8 employees and had to move out of Jim's house. The company grew an average of 46 percent each year, and after 6 years became a $6 million company. They have also started three other companies servicing the printing needs of other markets.

The difference...packaging?

How did Jim and Ken build the company? The service they provide isn't different from anything that's already out there. In fact, unlike other printing companies, Color for Real Estate requires full payment before your job even gets looked at. So, what's different? Their packaging. Packaging? They are a printer, how could packaging have anything to do with it? Everything at Color for Real Estate is packaged in fun. That's it. Simple. Business really doesn't have to be complicated. Many in this market are professional, but no one else in this market is fun.

Jim summed it up this way: "Two companies offer identical services and one makes you smile and the other one doesn't. Which would you do business with?" Color for Real Estate does all its business through its catalog. Jim said that he can't think of any other catalog that ever made him laugh. Ever. So, with his humor attitude it was not difficult to be different. Each year customers look forward to his new catalog. Darren is looking forward to it, too. Why? Because it's fun. Do you think that makes it more likely to be read? Sounds like the company is successfully using the Cannoli Principle and Michelle's Rule!

How does Jim make the catalog fun? All year he collects anything that amuses him and throws it in a box. Then Jim packs up his laptop and his humor box and heads to the beach to write. That's right, the beach (a lot more of a creative atmosphere than a corporate cubicle or boardroom). A whole year's worth of things that amuse you can add up to a very valuable box.

One of Jim's goals is to be a "bright spot" in the day of his clients. Not too many companies think this way. Simple and powerful strike again. He achieves this goal in many different ways. Being a "bright spot" is not only in line with having fun, but also a great way to look at building a stronger relationship with the customer.

22 Pounds of Personalized Pads and a Pathetic Surprise Prize!

Wow, that's a tongue twister! Actually, that was Jim's latest promotion. It was called, An Unexpected Tongue-Twister Special!

Companies that use direct mail promotion know that a 1 percent response rate is average and 3 percent is great. Color for Real Estate had just purchased a new printing press and wanted to put it to work right away. Did they ever! The new press became used solely for handling response to this promotion, running three shifts, and at the time of this interview it had been running non-stop for over three months. Because of an eye-catching title, a need for the product, the curiosity factor, and already-strong customer relationships, this promotion pulled upwards of a 15 percent response. For this company, those are very common numbers.

Jim believes if they had offered a regular 80-pad special, the response would not have been outstanding. Besides, "22 pounds" sounds more impressive. When you are servicing people who deal with the general public, some days can be easier than others. In this case, a pathetic toy prize surprise can bring a chuckle and a smile. Darren loved the fact that it was called a "pathetic" prize. If it had been called just a "surprise" prize, people could be disappointed. When you use Humble Humor and make fun of yourself, expectations are low, so there can be no letdown. An interesting note about using humor in promotions: Jim told Darren that no one has ever asked to be taken off their mailing list. That's powerful stuff!

Oh yeah, you want to know what the pathetic surprise prize was? It was a plastic nose pencil sharpener. You stick the pencil up the nose in order to sharpen it. Many of the employees thought that the sharpener would offend people. Jim said that they actually got many calls from people who loved them and enjoyed giving them to their kids.

Doing the unthinkable!

Every company experiences busy times and slower times. Companies vary greatly in how they handle the extra volume. Some offer overtime and others offer massages to overworked employees. How many intentionally decide to shut down?

Color for Real Estate gets extremely busy 6 or 7 times a year, and at the height of the mayhem, the presses stop, the phones shut down, and the entire staff actively engages in fun. An outgoing message on the phone tells customers that they are overwhelmed and the bosses want to give the staff a break and take them out for a few hours. "Most customers are very understanding," Jim said confidently. "They can relate to being overwhelmed and just call back later or the next day."

What do they do? Jim and Ken take the entire staff bowling, on picnics, out to press apple cider, and then come back and dive into fresh apple pie! Jim loves to challenge himself and come up with new and fun company adventures each time. Jim is proving to his people how important they are and how much he appreciates them. That is why Jim does it. The added benefit he gets from it? Once they do go back to work, Jim says, productivity skyrockets. Not a bad benefit for all concerned during the busiest times of the year.

Ooops!

Customers actually call up and say, "Just wanted to tell you, you guys are great." That does not come easily to a company. We've all heard that a customer problem is an opportunity. This overused statement is almost right. What we believe is that a customer problem is an opportunity to use self-effacing humor. This helps to keep the customer and build a stronger relationship. The link between stress and humor has been apparent since the early days of theater when it began to be symbolized by the classic comedy/tragedy masks. It's no coincidence that you always see these masks together. You can rarely have one without the other. The problem is that typical business professionals lack the ability to apply the other face, comedy, in their world.

The most logical place where self-effacing humor can apply is with customer service. Self-effacing works best in this situation because poking a little fun at yourself humanizes you, and customers are more willing to forgive and come back again. How does Color for Real Estate do this? When a mistake is made, regardless of who was at fault, they send out a full-color postcard that depicts an orangutan covering its mouth and looking sheepish. The caption reads, "What was I thinking? I'm so embarrassed."

On the reverse side, a brief letter reads,

Sorry for our goof! Enclosed are your reprints along with a very special prize selected just for you. Just our small (and amusing) way of saying thanks for being so understanding. Once again, sorry for the goof. Your support means a lot everything to us. Customer care, We take it personally.

See ya,
Jamie Pollard,
Prime Minister of Customer Service

Jamie makes things happen, and he makes sure his staff follows through with the company policy of making no excuses to customers. Using this as an example, what could you and your company do in this area?

OK, let's get personal

Color for Real Estate is unique in another way. They get personal. They have a full-time employee who has only one responsibility. They affectionately call her Nana. Every time someone places an order, she hand-writes a thank-you note. Even the customers who order every week still get that handwritten note. Talk about humanizing. That's a lot of thank-you notes! Jim feels that the personal touch is important and buys a lot of loyalty. It is something he is willing to pay for every time. No wonder they don't need to spend money on advertising!

Real humane-atarians

An unexpected quality that humor-using companies have in common is that of giving back to the community. Most such companies are very charitable. Color for Real Estate and its employees help out at the local humane society. They also produce all of the advertisements and printing for the humane society at no charge. Loving animals does not stop there. Jim's golden retriever, Timber, is pictured in their catalog. Timber comes to work each day, and all the employees are encouraged to bring their pets to work. One of the employees told Darren that they have lost more than one sandwich by leaving it unattended, but they find that having the dogs around is very therapeutic.

How do employees feel?

When potential customers request a catalog, Jim sends out a letter that states, "A lot has changed since 'the basement days,' but a lot hasn't. When I hired our first employee, I tacked up a crudely written sign that I thought might keep us focused. Today it still hangs in our Customer Service Department...." The letter includes this list:

TOP 10 RULES TO LIVE BY

1. Follow the Golden Rule with our customers and with our co-workers.
2. The friendship and trust of our customers is our most valuable asset—guard it.
3. Let's not take ourselves too seriously.
4. Under promise and over deliver.
5. Listen more than you speak. New ideas will come from our REALTORS®, if we listen.
6. Never sell REALTORS® anything which we aren't totally convinced can help them.
7. When we mess up (and we will), apologize, tell the unvarnished truth, make no excuses, and make it right, right away.
8. Bring your pets to work. A whole day is too long to be without companionship.
9. Volunteer in the community one week a year on company time.
10. Connect with customers. Take their feedback to heart.

This is not the average game plan. Many companies use humor in advertisements just to get noticed and entice business, but here the beauty is more than skin deep. A working environment based on these ethics and guidelines is a positive one. It shows in the attitudes of the employees. Darren could not resist the opportunity to interview a couple of the employees during his tour of the facility.

As mentioned in "Wait Management," Darren's first live exposure to Color for Real Estate was over the phone, placing an order with Karen. In his original conversation, before she knew who he was, Darren asked if she liked her job. Without hesitation she enthusiastically replied, "Omigosh, you don't know how fortunate I feel to have found this place." How would your employees candidly respond? Why?

Jim was asked to leave the room during these interviews. The people Darren spoke to were so sincere. They could not say enough about Jim and were quick to say that how they are treated is why they are willing to work hard every day. They also said that when talking with friends they always get the question, "Do they need any help?" What do you think your people say about work to their closest friends? Keri, who formerly co-managed a front desk at a resort, said, "This was the best work decision I ever made." How much would you pay for that kind of loyalty? The nice thing is that it isn't as much about the pay as it is about the environment and how the employees are treated.

The employees love the fact that they are empowered and encouraged to admit company mistakes. Karen, formerly employed at a car dealership, said, "We are given the leverage to do what it takes to put a smile on the customer's face, and we have no stress to have to give people *a line.*" This leeway, and lack of pressure from management, seemed of the utmost importance to the people on the front lines. They also mentioned that it is tough to stay in a bad mood around their co-workers. This is truly a Funsucker-free environment.

When Darren asked staff directly how they felt they were treated, they replied, "You gotta love it!" Jim wants his people to be comfortable. He even said, "I don't care if they come to work in their pajamas, as long as they do a good job." Jim claims he's the luckiest guy in the world. Employees think he's pretty cool, too!

Hiring humor...2 questions

Prospective employees are asked to read the Color for Real Estate fan mail. How enthusiastic is your company fan mail? Do you get any? They call it the "We Are So Fabulous Book." They believe that fan mail tells much more about the people who run the business than a fancy company brochure ever would.

When word got out about how Jim and Ken treat their employees, everyone wanted (and still wants) to work there. As we've said before, some jobs are so fun that employees are willing to make less money for the job. Jim and Ken, on the other hand, pay more than equivalent jobs elsewhere pay. The "books" are even open to all employees.

When Color for Real Estate is hiring new employees, Jim asks only two questions. The first is, "What are you passionate about?" They run an honest business and want only honest people working there. Jim believes that if candidates answer the question with something about work, or doing a good job, they are probably not being genuine. The second question is, "How many gas stations are there in the United States?" No kidding! If the candidate makes no attempt to solve this problem, how are they going to be able to attempt to solve the day-to-day problems that arise?

Surprisingly enough, the new hire turnover at Color for Real Estate is actually very high. Jim responds by pointing out that even though they have fun and treat their people right, they expect hard work and enthusiasm in return. It is usually very evident within the first three months who is (and is not) cut out to work there. The long-term employee retention is a different story. In the long-term, the turnover is nil! That's right—none, zip, zero, nada!

Why don't more companies do business this way? Rick and Darren can't answer that one. They hope success stories such as these begin to change that. For those who already believe in the *Laugh & Get Rich* philosophy it is easier to stand out in the crowd the way Jim and his $200-a-day start-up company did. The original feedback Jim and Ken received—that "some people won't get it" and some "will be offended"—was right on, but so was their plan. Jim and Ken seem to really enjoy what they do and how they do it. Bottom line—you can't argue with success.

One of Jim's goals was to build a company that was not average. Since average companies are not built on the "foundation of fun," Jim's company will never be average. This just proves there is room in any humor-deprived industry for a new leader. Jim said there is no aspect of his business that humor doesn't touch. It all comes back to the quote that opened this chapter, which Rick affectionately calls Laffey's Line: "Humor is the most underrated and overlooked value-added service you could provide...and costs you nothing."

RECAP:

- Packaging? Jim says, "Two companies offer identical services and one makes you smile and the other one doesn't. Which would you do business with?"

- No humor in your industry? What an opportunity!

- "22 Pounds of Personalized Pads and A Pathetic Surprise Prize!" or "Memo Pad Special!" Attention is the first step in the sales process.

- Selling and customer service are important areas to profit from humor over the long haul.

- Self-effacing Humble Humor works great at relieving customer service tension and keeping customers.

- How would your front-line employees respond to someone asking them if they like their job?

- How can you Get Personal?

- Humor your customers—you might get fan mail, too.

- Zero to $6 million in 6 years. Enough said!

Ideas this gives you for your business:

_____

_____

_____

_____

_____

_____

PART V

PUTTING IT ALL TOGETHER

CHAPTER 44

The Nifty Fifty

50 Tips, Techniques, and Strategies to Laugh & Get Rich

"Exhilaration is that feeling you get just after a great idea hits you, and before you realize what's wrong with it."

– The Best of BITS & PIECES

This chapter is designed as a reference or glossary of some of the best ways to add humor, fun, or playful activity into your work—to help you do more business. Some of the ideas listed here are detailed in other chapters. Others only appear in this chapter. So here we go!

Humor can be the default. In any situation, from meetings to sales presentations, consider fun as your first response. Understand that anything can be humorized, but the first step is to be aware of it and then use it.

1) The Business Letter: Have some fun with your letters. Think funny. Say what the other person is thinking. Use short paragraphs, all capital letters, underlined phrases, and always have a fun PS. These letters get an immediate result.

Ever have a situation where you needed an answer and conventional messages weren't getting any response? Rick was trying to find out if a sales woman would represent this book to the library market. After several traditional phone messages Rick wrote the following letter:

> Rebecca,
>
> I hadn't heard from you so I quickly assumed you hated my book, Laugh & Get Rich. But just when I was ready to jump out the window in sheer desperation, I had the thought. She might be on vacation! Then I said, "NO, she must be on a selling trip and is trying to focus on selling books she already represents."
>
> That sounded better, but then I said to myself, "Rick you are rationalizing again. If she really liked the book she would have been hot to call us but she didn't, so go ahead and jump."
>
> So I did.
>
> But I'm on the first floor and there is a grassy knoll outside the window and it's impossible to hurt yourself. So now I have a pair of grass-stained pants and I am still wondering if you liked, or hated the book. So the reason why I am writing is because we are thinking of moving to the third floor... and if you decide to reject the book I would much rather you do it soon while we are still on the first floor.
>
> Look forward to hearing from you soon,
> Rick Segel, CSP
>
> PS. Hopefully, you liked that way of responding. We believe it is part of the Laugh & Get Rich Philosophy of doing business. If you found it fun and amusing, then you are right for the book. If you didn't, we aren't right for each other. Hopefully, you liked it.

Rick got a call the morning after she received the letter.

2) The Memo and E-Mail: The same rules apply as the letter, just in shorter version. Look for the areas you can apply the "humor twist." It could be a play on words, an association to a current event, or even responding literally to what the other person says.

What fonts do you use? Instead of using boring type faces, such as we are using here (that's a perfect example of saying what you are thinking type of humor), use a cartoon style or any other offbeat style. It will set the mood.

3) Illustrations: These might include clip art, a cartoon, or just a happy face. They can change a tone and a feeling from serious to fun. In Chapter 43, Color for Real Estate illustrates the use of this technique with a few one-liners interspersed throughout the catalog to make it fun.

4) Color: This just doesn't apply to communications, it applies to everything! Black, brown, and navy aren't fun colors. Red, yellow, and bright blue are fun colors. You could send out a death notice in yellow and red, and everyone would want to come to the funeral because they would think it was going to be fun. Yes, we are exaggerating, but you get the point.

5) Conversational Language: Do you know where we are coming from on this one? Write like you speak. When your language is easy to understand, it is user-friendly. Rick was acknowledged by the Des Moines Register as one of the best consultants the state used for his consulting report, because it was written in plain, easy-to-understand English. Everyone else wrote in "consultantese." (Actually, Rick would have written it another way but he didn't know any other way.)

6) Renaming: This is the art of giving people fun, playful names. Instead of Rick, it could be Rick a-doodle. Rick has a friend who is the master of "renaming." Names he has created all relate to some funny association to the person. Names such as Bo Bo, Lumpy, Ragu, and his favorite Newman. Which comes from a person being the "new man" at the company. Three years later he is affectionately referred to as Newman. His purpose for doing it is to let them know he is a fun loving guy. One word of caution, the name should always lift a person up, rather than bringing someone down. These are fun names not hurtful names. That's the ultimate bonding—when you become the person who gave a big vendor a nickname.

7) Fun Facts: Or this could even be called Fun Fax because that is exactly what it is. A monthly one-sheet fax sent to your customers listing the holidays for the month, a cartoon, a few short quotes, a non-offensive joke or two, and in one of the lower corners of the page a small ad about your company. It doesn't have to be about a promotional item. It can just say that this fax is brought to you by, and then list your company. It is just a wonderful way to keep in touch with your customers and have them look forward to receiving this fax from you.

8) Invitations: What Will You Write Them On? It's not always what you say, it might be the form of the invitation that makes it special and fun. This includes techniques like writing on a brown paper lunch bag for a bag lunch meeting or writing on a coffee mug for a breakfast meeting. The best one Rick ever saw was for a meeting of the branch employees of a bank. They wanted to show off their newly remodeled facilities to their employees. Part of the remodel included new employee bathrooms which were long overdue and a source of constant complaints for years. The bank president sent out invitations on toilet paper. The message was in good taste, but it did announce the ceremonial first flush that would signify a new page in the bank's history. He even decorated the water closet with flowers. It was his way of saying, "OK, I listened to you and corrected a problem. Now let's laugh it off and move on."

9) Fun "Thank You" Gifts: This is any type of gift that makes you smile. Rick just received a small box of brownies from the Fat Witch Bakery. It came in the cutest box and was just a happy gift. Rick likes to send bouquets of candy. Darren once sent an oversized aspirin to a client who mentioned having a tension headache. The twelve inch aspirin is passed around for the office "headache of the day." (See Chapter 30, The 3 Most Powerful Questions)

10) Oooops—Fixing mistakes: Darren's friend, Renee, called him in a panic one night. She had made a terrible mistake during an important interview. In the midst of sending a follow up "Thank You" to her potential employer, she inadvertently used the wrong name. Ouch! Darren suggested that she admit it and make light of the mistake. This is the e-mail she wrote after talking to Darren:

Connie,

Hmmm, here's how I would grade how it is going so far:

+ 10 spelling and pronouncing awkward company name correctly

+ 10 matching skill set

+ 10 passion, commitment and desire

+ 10 good rapport and conversation on interview

−4000 giving interviewer a whole different name than her parents gave her upon birth

This is one of life's embarrassing moments. I am truly sorry. I am still extremely interested in working with your team and I hope that you will still consider me a viable candidate.

Renee

The interviewer had fun with her response as well. She said she loved honesty, and appreciated the humor at her own expense! Bottom line—Renee got the job.

11) Telephone Chatter: Instead of the normal, dry business call, have some fun with the person who answers the phone. Don't just ask for your party. Celebrate the fact you didn't get an answering machine. "You are a real person! This is wonderful. Today is my lucky day. Maybe I'll even play the lottery today." Just make sure the person is receptive to this type of kidding. Some people might not like it, but most people love dealing with positive people and using humor.

12) Telephone Messages: This is the difference between getting a call back or not—leave fun messages, especially with voice mail. Look at it this way: it is a 15 second radio commercial, and there are plenty of things that can be said and remembered within 15 seconds. Once when Rick received a message on a machine that said, "You've reached the BAT line-leave a message." It sounded to him that they must have had a good sense of humor. So Rick left a message saying, "Before Batman and Robin slide down the bat pole, call me." And Rick did get a call back. That's when we both got a good laugh because Rick had called the Big And Tall Association.

13) Meetings: Meeting were made for fun and playful behavior. You can be just as effective with fun, even more so than by delivering a dry message. Have the time fly by. The following are a few examples:

14) Dress Up: At a memorable meeting of the top executives of a company the president came to the meeting wearing a Superman outfit. His other key executives were wearing super hero costumes as well. (See Chapter 6, The Clown Concept for more details)

15) Improvisation at a Meeting: As opposed to delivering the normal, dry content, let your employees act out fun scenarios to help clarify a point that you are trying to make. (See Chapter 27, The Humor Detour)

16) Candid Camera Principle: This tactic involves putting people into unusual situations. Have these scenarios filmed and shown later at a company outing or gathering. One memorable situation occurred at a buffet table when people's heads came through the table made-up to look like heads of lettuce. The reaction from the people getting food went from shock to hysteria. Another great place to put a camera is in front or on top of the office refrigerator. And it even gets better if you can have the refrigerator talk to the person who is opening it. (See Chapter 22, Rule of the Unexpected)

17) Impostoring: This is when a professional speaker, comedian, or actor speaking at a meeting portrays someone else. An example is when Rick impostored for AARP and pretended to be a Washington bureaucrat unveiling new regulations effecting seniors. Once the audience got past the new rules and regulations which were fictitious, they had one of the best laughs ever.

18) Joke of the Day: Post a new joke every day for customers, employees, or both. It gets the day started off with a smile. Some companies even put the joke of the day on their voice mail messages.

19) Quote of the Day: This is similar to the Joke of the Day, but the difference is that there is no punch line. It is intended for companies that wouldn't dare have a joke of the day.

20) Signage: This comes in all different sizes and varieties, but regardless of the size, the goal and purpose are the same—to bring a smile or laugh to the reader and to have that smile or laugh associated with the company. These are our favorites:

- A sign on the main highway for the Big Dig construction project in Boston that was intended to relieve tension. It said, "Rome wasn't built in a day. If it were, we would have used their contractor."

- A sign for a health club that said, "Are you fat and ugly? Do you just want to be ugly? Join the West End Gym."

21) In Chapter 35 we discuss Mac The Pig: This is a great example of the use of humor in signage to create word of mouth advertising. If you want word of mouth advertising, give them something to talk about.

22) Creative menus: As with putting in side-comments or fun illustrations in a newsletter, they work just as effectively on a restaurant menu. It helps to set the mood. How about "renaming" the food to your theme or local area?

23) In Negotiations: Rick believes that negotiations are the best place to use humor. First, negotiations are always easier if the other party likes you. Humor helps to get the other party to like you. Second, where humor is such a great tension reliever, it works well in the heat of negotiations to remove the tension. It creates what we refer to as the "mini humor vacation." And lastly, humor can cover up a failed attempt at asking for more. (See Chapter 36, Negotiating Humor Homework)

24) Crazy Hat Day: This is something that can be done with just your employees to set a fun, playful mood for the day. You obviously want to give a prize to the winner. It says that we care about you as a person as well as an employee and that we are part of a big family. This also works as a retail promotion to get customers in a festive, buying mood.

25) Joy Gang: This is a committee of the fun, spirited people within your company. They meet on a regular basis to look for ways to add fun and humor in business. The term was created at Ben & Jerry's Ice Cream, but has been duplicated by hundreds of other companies very effectively. The purpose is to increase sales and productivity through fun and playful activities.

26) The Humor / Creativity Room: This is a room in your company that will be brightly decorated and will have joke books, humor books, humor videos, Laugh & Get Rich, some sofas, tables, and chairs to create a perfect brainstorming environment where creativity rules. One company even put a non-functioning toilet seat in the middle of the room because one member of the team said that he got his best ideas on the "john." Remember as you're thinking funny, you are thinking creatively.

27) Tootsie Rolls®: Over the course of the years, I have seen a few salespeople give out tootsie rolls every time they made a stop. One even built the reputation of being called the Tootsie Roll® King. It's a fun trademark that everyone likes and it associates you with fun because Tootsie Rolls® have that image. M&Ms® and Snickers® also work well. However the best one I ever saw was a dental lab that gave out Tootsie Rolls® to all of their dentists. It might seem a bit unusual but not to him. His response is, "I'm just promoting business!"

28) Product Differentiation: Change the rules of engagement. Compete on fun as opposed to competing on price, service, or even quality. Consider fun. The best example of that is Pike's Fish Market in Seattle. Fish are a commodity and every fish store sells almost the same product. However at Pikes, they made a science of having fun. Their playful behavior draws big crowds and the word of mouth advertising has built a business that has become so famous that a training video has been made about this business. A book about this fish market has become a best seller. Almost every product can be differentiated with humor. The best part is that the focus is away from price.

29) Cannoli Principle of Attraction: This principle is from Chapter 31 where we illustrate the use of a fun character to deliver a sales message. In this case it was the Cannoli Brothers—two fun-loving Mafia misfit types who could sell almost anything. Children's products use cartoon characters. Create your own personality. Dunkin' Donuts used a man named Fred for years. When he retired the whole chain gave away free coffee for a day. What publicity! Try it. It works!

30) Boring Instructions: If you have boring instructions you have to share with customers or the public, add a humorous twist. Have some fun with it. Joke about how boring it is. You will just be saying what people are already thinking. This is one strategy that built Southwest Airlines and they used it with their fun, safety instruction messages.

31) Company Policies Written with A Humorous Twist: This is the same as the boring instructions, just expanded to include company policies. Actually, any dry or boring information could probably use a little levity—that is, if you want people to understand and listen.

32) Comedy Classes: Teach the team to be funny by having lunch at a comedy club. Most comedy clubs are closed during the day, but many are available for private parties. They will supply comedians who will share secrets with your team. This is generally very inexpensive and an experience you will never forget. There are also classes offered at junior colleges and adult educational programs.

33) Humor Buddies: Have a friend that you share jokes, gags, and stories with—someone who will tell you when the joke or story is good to use or not. Or when you need a little help with a punch line or a suggestion on just the right word to use. Many times a fresh set of eyes can find humor in something others can't, but what makes a buddy truly valuable is knowing your style of delivering material, or just the way you think.

34) The Magic Shop: Go to your local magic shop and look for a few gags or tricks you can use in different situations. People who work at magic shops are generally very willing to help you find something that will work for you. This is great if you are not naturally funny. You will become a conduit for fun because of your tricks. This is great for networking!

35) Listen to a Comedy Tape: Listening to a comedy tape will help you to think in a humorous way. Not that you will use the material you hear. That doesn't work. It is to inspire you to come up with the type of humor that works for you.

36) Listen to a Comedy Tape More than Once: We listen the first time to make us laugh. The second time is to find out why we laugh. This is valuable information to have because there might be things you don't find funny that the rest of the world finds hilarious.

37) Inclusionary Humor: This term means to always include people in the joke or the laughter. There is nothing more aggravating then having a group of people laughing in front of you, but you don't know why they are laughing. (See Chapter 21, The Auntie Factor)

38) Price Deflection: This is one of the very best applications for fun and laughter in business and it can be used several ways. The first is by focusing on the fun over the price. Disney and Pikes Market are great examples of all of that. Next time you are negotiating or discussing price, just giggle a little when anyone gives you an offer. That's all you have to do. They will think something is wrong and will either raise the bid, withdraw, or think they have insulted you. Most of time the other person will raise their offer. The other strategy is to just have fun with the price. When someone asks you what your best price is always quote 30% higher. When they say that's not the best price simply say, "It is for me." They will laugh and you may have distracted them enough. But if not, handle it with fun because when we are too emotional, it doesn't work.

39) Greeting: We all know a positive greeting is good, but have a fun and interesting greeting ready when someone asks the traditional question, like "How are you doing?" On the phone or in person, Darren's energetically replies, "Not bad for a bald guy!" The humor is directed at himself. Rick likes to say, "Great! The Red Sox didn't lose." He will say terrible if they lost. Being a Red Sox fan brings out humor and compassion from people around the world considering they haven't won a championship since 1918. The line is funnier in January when they aren't playing. We know a sales rep who always answers the "how are you" question with, "Terrible, my gold fish passed away." It has become his trademark. Whenever anyone sees this man, they always ask about his goldfish.

40) Exaggeration: This is a basic technique in using humor where we make something bigger than life. When we exaggerate size or length of time to the point of being comical, it creates a humorous situation that will usually get a laugh.

41) Similarities: This technique is outlined extensively in Chapter 29, Make Wit Not War. It is one of Darren's favorite tools to find the nuggets of humor for a presentation, but it works anywhere you want to find funny material. Make a list of words about two different topics and finding the comparisons, such as growing a garden and raising children. The weeds are always going to pop up. This works all the time.

42) The Save: This is the remark you use after you tell a joke or story that doesn't work. Something like, "I thought it was funny when Charlie gave it to me." Charlie might be famous for telling bad jokes. Johnny Carson built a career with saves. It is simply acknowledging that something didn't work and throwing in a little self-deprecating humor to get the laugh.

43) Self-Deprecating Humor: This is when you make yourself the butt or target of the joke. This is the safest type of humor you can use because the only one who can get offended is you. Another benefit of self-deprecating humor is that it makes the other person feel more important.

44) Ugly Tie: Rick always wears an ugly Tabasco tie when he speaks. He does that to break the ice with the people he meets. Many people will comment on his tie. (He is wearing it on the cover of this book.) In the middle of his talk he will discuss the significance of the tie. He tells everyone that he hates the tie, but he uses it to facilitate networking by becoming a conversation piece. Ties are not worn today as much as they used to be, but the concept works just as well with buttons or T-shirts.

45) Game Show Training: This is the most fun you can have in training today, especially if you have a competitive group of people. The way it works is to use a game show format such as Jeopardy, Family Feud, or the old College Bowl. Even with Jeopardy you can play with 5 person teams. People will remember more information while they are having a ball playing the game. You must supply some type of prizes. You can buy the board games or create the games in a Powerpoint format. This is a lot of fun!

46) Holiday's ala Chase's: Chase's Calendar of Events is probably the best source of crazy holidays and birthdays to celebrate. It is a large reference book found in most public library reference sections. This book can be used to create fun promotions as well as crazy days to celebrate at your business. Examples include: "Dump Your Significant Jerk Day," or Thomas Crapper's Birthday, the inventor of the flush toilet (January 23rd), or even Laugh and Get Rich Day (February 8th). If you call the creators of the day, they will send you information about their day and why it was created.

47) Wait Management: Humor is at its best when it is used to help relieve stress. One thing that seems to generate stress is when we are forced to wait. Waiting is bad enough, but why are we always forced to wait in the most boring of surroundings? This is an opportunity to WOW a customer by entertaining them during the waiting process. Many places, such as airline terminals, have started to figure this out and have added TV monitors with CNN playing. Our attitude is to go beyond the TV set and try to make the wait more enjoyable and fun. (See Chapter 25, Wait Management)

48) Office: Why do offices and waiting rooms have to be so boring? Liven them up with bright colors and things to do. Imagine a TV playing classic comedy tapes. You'll enjoy the wait and be in a good mood when you have your meeting.

49) Lines are Opportunities: Rick hates to wait, especially in lines. He wants to be entertained and made to feel good while he is waiting. Theme parks do a great job with this, but nothing is as good as a person who makes you laugh while you are waiting.

50) On Hold: Make your message fun. It puts people in good moods and has them talking about you. That's how you create word-of-mouth advertising.

Have fun! Let these ideas spur your own!

CHAPTER 45

Summing It All Up
Whew!

"When one journey ends, another begins."

– Rick Segel

As we sit down for the last rewrite of the last chapter, ending this four-year journey, we reflect upon the struggle we had putting this book together.

It isn't easy having two people come together with different backgrounds, different points of view, and different agendas for a work such as this. Agreeing on what was important was probably the greatest struggle of all. After all, Darren is younger, single, from the corporate world, and Rick is older, married with a family, and has been running his own business for 30 years.

The single common denominator that brings the two together is the belief that humor works. Rick is naturally funny, while Darren has to work to get his laughs. Darren understands why his audience is laughing while Rick only cares that they are laughing. Humor is the bond between the two and it is the bond between people all over the world.

Rick recently spoke in Istanbul, Turkey, and found that many of his stories that illustrate frustration on the job and with families are universal, producing the same laughs in the same spots even with translation. Laughter and humor are a gift but they are also tools for life, for living, and a way of doing business that has been around for centuries—just referred to in other terms. Maybe it was called breaking the ice, or connecting with the customer, or even softening up the prospect. It is now time to call it what it really is: using humor as a tool to help make a sale.

Is this wrong? Is it manipulative? We don't think so, because the world has changed, even in the short four years since we started this project. Companies are no longer the exception in using laughter or humor as the company attitude. They are part of a new wave of informality. Dress down days have become dress down everydays. Creative, fun memos are no longer the WOW! they once were. In the words of one of the great philosophers of our time, Bob Dylan, "The times, they are a-changing."

The revolution has already begun, and although this book might have been started to signal the start of a new revolution, its purpose now is to convince the last stalwarts that humor works as a business tool. We also want to say thanks to the visionaries we interviewed who were called crazy for adopting such radical ideas. They made the way we do business a little more widely accepted. They also gave us great real-life examples to share.

No longer are companies just selling the product. The customer can get the product anywhere today. We are all just a few mouse clicks away from whatever we want. We are now selling the experience, and the experience must be easy, hassle-free, and fun. We have reached an age of entertainment in doing business. We have reached the era of laughing and getting rich. We have gone from a time of companies with names like Amalgamated or Enterprise to Yahoo! and Go.com. We have finally become user-friendly, but we still strive to be successful (using money as the benchmark of success).

As a last request, we hope that the money you make from using these techniques filters back into your community, to our environment, and to the less fortunate who might need a little extra help. We assure you that a portion of the sale of this book will find its way to places and people that make a difference in our world. We hope we have made a difference in yours.

"If you hear a voice within you saying
'you are not a painter' then by all means paint...
And that voice will be silenced."
— Vincent Van Gogh

For those naysayers who cannot see how humor belongs in business...this book is the painting that silences the voice.

Several stories and ideas in this book have many parallels. This is intentional. It is part of learning and relating. We could have made the book shorter, and instead we chose to make it more effective. Some stories will be more helpful than others, but they all are working together to give you a better understanding of how humor works in business and how it can contribute to your bottom line.

Make it fun and they will come

The analogy about humor in business that comes to mind is fishing. Think about why people go fishing? Why do they? Why do they spend so much money and effort on raising fish to stock ponds and rivers for the sport? Why don't they just take out the middle man, the lake? Go and buy your fish at the store. Much more cost-efficient. Wouldn't it save time and effort? Darren's dad would lose much of his enjoyment. It's about the act of fishing. In business, it is the fun. If you make it fun, they will come. Not just customers, employees too!

There you have it. Real-life examples of tools and the people who use humor capitalistically. It's up to you now. How is this going to change the way you think? What ideas did it generate? What are you going to do about them? Its been said by many people: "If you go on doing what you've been doing, you'll keep on getting what you've been getting."

If you change nothing, this book was for entertainment purposes only. In that case, we hope it was worth the price. You know your business. Only you can figure out what might work for you. When you bought the book you bought into the philosophy. You could have purchased many others—why this one? You spent your money based on the title and subject matter, proving you are one of us.

How can you use your own beliefs to help you *Laugh & Get Rich?*

References

The Forbes Book of Business Quotations, Ted Goodman (Editor), Black Dog & Leventhal Publishers, 1997.

Think and Grow Rich, Napoleon Hill, Wilshire Book Company, 1999.

The Wall Street Journal, Dec. 13, 1995, by Dana Milbank, article about Mark Katz.

Home Office Computing, ISSN: 0899-7373, Bernadette Grey, Hugh Roome, 555 Broadway, NY, NY, 10012.

Meet the Authors

Rick Segel, CSP, a seasoned retailer of 25 years, owned one of New England's most successful independent woman's specialty stores. He is a contributing writer for numerous international publications and a founding member of the Retail Advisory Council for Johnson & Wales University. Rick is the director of Retail Training for the Retail Association of Massachusetts and is currently serving on the Boards of Directors for five corporations and associations.

Rick is a Certified Speaking Professional (CSP), the highest earned designation from the National Speakers Association. Rick is past president of the New England Speakers Association (a chapter of NSA) and one of the most awarded speakers in New England. He has been a featured speaker in 43 states and three continents, and has delivered over 1,200 presentations. Rick's clients include Shell Oil Company, Dollar Tree Stores, Dillards, San Francisco International Gift Fair, and the Department of State and Regional Development of New South Wales, Australia.

Rick has authored 5 audio programs, two training videos, two books including *Retail Business Kit for Dummies*, part of the "Dummies Series" and is the on-line marketing expert for Staples.com.

To find out more about Rick's available products or to see what he can do for your organization, contact him at:

Rick Segel & Associates
One Wheatland St., Burlington, MA 01803
781-272-9995 phone • 781-272-9996 fax
Rick@RickSegel.com
www.RickSegel.com

LEARNING RESOURCES BY RICK SEGEL

AUDIO CASSETTES
How To Make Your Retail Business Profitable – This brand new 6 cassette audio program explores every aspect of the retail business. It uncovers the secrets to profitability and creates an easy to use step-by-step approach that can turn any store into a profit producing business entity. $59.95

BOOKS
Retail Business Kit for Dummies – This 384-page book is the most complete guide to retailing today. It explores every aspect of the retail business and also includes a CD-ROM filled with forms, checklists, and guides to make retailing easier. $29.95

Awkward Moments...Celebrating the Humor in Life's Uncomfortable Situations – This book is a humorous look at life and all those silly, awkward, embarrassing moments that can ruin our self-esteem if not handled with humor. It includes 40 cartoon illustrations and numerous stories that will tickle your funny bone while putting life into the proper perspective. $11.95

VIDEOS
Effective Suggestive Selling—Did You See This? – This 60-minute video highlights an easy to use system that increases sales wherever it is used. It breaks the ice, facilitates multiple sales, and makes closing sales a simple. $49.95

Stop Losing Retail Sales – This 60-minute video is the perfect training video for sales personnel and their managers. It is comprised of short vignettes of do's and don'ts in customer service and sales. $49.95

LEARNING SYSTEMS AND MANUALS
How to Run A Sale – This how-to, step-by-step manual reveals the secrets of the sale professionals and will increase your sales results significantly. $19.95

Open To Thrive – A revolutionary way to look at Open to Buy. It is comprised on an audio cassette and a tracker for sales, inventory, and cash flow. $29.95

Darren LaCroix is a rare corporate comedian. He is considered a pioneer at writing and delivering speeches due to his technique of "customizing" humor. He unearths common frustrations and occupational pet peeves about individual organizations giving him ammunition to make audiences laugh from their toes. His clean cut humor and personalized attention truly make him unique in the meetings industry.

Darren's success is remarkable since he was considered *Least Likely to Be Funny* in high school. Without a funnybone in his body, but a willingness to fail and a desire to learn, he pursued his dream. He first took the comedy stage in 1992 at an "open mike nite" in Boston. Though he bombed Darren became a student of comedy reading every book, taking every class, and grabbing every chance at stage time he could get. Darren is living proof that humor is a skill that can be learned.

His unique background inspired the creation of *The Humor Boot Camp*. Darren, Rick, and comedian Dave Fitzgerald designed the program for anyone who gives presentations. It teaches professionals to be funnier and therefore, to be more effective. Darren is the host and producer of the audio learning program *Learn How the Pros MAKE 'EM LAUGH.*

Darren has also brought humor and inspiration to the world of healing. He produced a video documentary about his best friend, comedian/cancer survivor Dave Fitzgerald. This video program, *Living and Laughing with Cancer—A Comedian's Journey* won critical acclaim at the WorldFest Houston Film Festival.

To find out more about Darren's learning programs or to check his speaking availability please contact his office at:

The Humor Institute, Inc.
PO Box 557, Auburn, MA 01501
888-528-4451 phone • 888-820-2737 fax

e-mail: Darren@HumorInst.com
www.DarrenLaCroix.com
www.HumorBootCamp.com
www.HUMOR411.com

LEARNING RESOURCES BY DARREN LACROIX

AUDIO LEARNING PROGRAM
Learn How the Pros MAKE 'EM LAUGH
Do you sell or give presentations? Do you want to have more fun? Make your audience laugh! The myth is dispelled, you can learn how to be funnier. Your host, comedian Darren LaCroix was considered in high school to be the *least likely to ever be funny*. He is living proof that humor can be learned. Darren shares with listeners the wisdom of his comedy mentors through educational interviews. You will learn how to develop your own humor, deliver your messages more effectively, and bond with audiences. MAKE 'EM LAUGH offers secrets, step-by-step exercises, & advice from eight masters of humor.

4 CD Set with 23-page workbook $59.95
4 Cassette Set $49.95

HEALING/INSPIRATION
Healing, Hope, & Humor: A Survivor's Story
This 40-minute, award-winning program captures USO Comedian, Dave Fitzgerald's survivor attitude. Dave gives pratical advice and inspiration to people diagnosed with a life-threatening illness and their families. He also reminds viewers that *laughter is the best medicine* and lets you in on his healing prescription. This program is produced and hosted by Darren LaCroix founder of the Humor Institute.

VHS $24.95
Audio CD $19.95
Cassette $14.95

HUMOR
Healing Humor: I've Fallen and I CAN Get up!
USO Comedian Dave Fitzgerald live! Dave has appeared in Caroline's Comedy Hour and Evening at the Improv. This program is 30 minutes of uplifting, nonstop laughter caught on tape! Listen to Dave's wildly funny views on weight-loss, coffee addiction, and recovery from life threatening illness! You will never forget his famous "feel the breeze" story.

VHS $24.95
CD $19.95
Cassette $14.95
2 Video Set – Both videos $44.95

Areas of Concentration

Chapters to Review

Communication

Meetings

Networking/Relationship Building

Presentations

Selling

Teambuilding

Specific House Publishing
One Wheatland Street
Burlington, MA 01803

Specific House Publishing
Quick Order Form

Laugh & Get Rich
How to Profit from Humor in Any Business

Fax orders: (781) 272-9996

Phone orders: (781) 272-9995
Please have your credit card ready

Postal orders: Specific House Publishing,
One Wheatland St., Burlington, MA 01803

Please send me _____ copies of *Laugh & Get Rich* at $19.95 each, plus shipping and handling.

Name: _____

Address: _____

City: _____ State: _____ Zip: _____

Phone: _____

Email address: _____

Sales tax: Please add 5% for products shipped to Massachusetts addresses.

Shipping: US: $4 for the first book and $2 for each additional book. **International:** Based on ship-to location and current rates; please call for exact amounts.

Payment type: ❑ Check enclosed ❑ Credit card
❑ Visa ❑ Mastercard ❑ American Express

Credit card #: _____

Name on card: _____ exp date: ____ / ____

Please send more information on:
❑ Other books & learning products ❑ Speaking / seminars ❑ Consulting